T0194033

Who is God? Who is Jesus Christ?
Does God really love us? Who are we to God?
What is Life? What is death?
What happens when we die? Do we become angels?
Is there a Heaven? Is there a Hell?
Is God really going to destroy the world?
How can I be saved and live forever?

Many people today have a totally false concept of who God really is and what His plans are for the human race. God is not an angry and vengeful Deity who wants to destroy everyone who does not obey Him. In his new book, come with Pastor Michael Hunter as he takes you through the Bible to discover who we really are as beings and how much God and Jesus Christ really love us.

DANGEROUS JOURNEY HOME

A Prodigal Son's Journey back to Father God

MICHAEL HUNTER

authorHOUSE®

AuthorHouse™
1663 Liberty Drive
Bloomington, IN 47403
www.authorhouse.com
Phone: 833-262-8899

Published by AuthorHouse 08/05/2020

ISBN: 978-1-7283-6612-8 (sc)
ISBN: 978-1-7283-6610-4 (hc)
ISBN: 978-1-7283-6611-1 (e)

Library of Congress Control Number: 2020912044

Print information available on the last page.

CONTENTS

AUTHOR'S NOTES

Please do not skip over the Bible quotations dispersed throughout this book. The Scriptures are not there to help support the opinions of this book. The purpose of this book is to help the reader become more familiar with the Word of God. We cannot learn to love God's Word if we do not read it. Many of the Scriptures have been taken from the King James Version of the Bible because I have found it to generally be the most commonly available accurate translation of the original Hebrew and Greek manuscripts. I did keep in mind, however, that the King James Version of the Bible was written hundreds of years ago and contains many words and phrases that are now no longer in common usage. Therefore, for the purpose of clarity and ease of understanding, you will find that some passages are paraphrased (contain modern language) in order to help explain antiquated words and phrases. In doing this, every effort has been made to make certain that such paraphrases retain the integrity of the original Greek and Hebrew in order to ensure that nothing is added to or taken away from God's Word.

There are also numerous Bible quotes throughout this book that are taken from several other translations of the Bible simply because I believe that they offer the clearest and most accurate modern language translation of that particular passage, expressing the Word of God in a way that is easy for everyone to understand while maintaining the integrity of the original Hebrew and Greek Scriptures. Greek and Hebrew definitions have been sourced from Strong's Exhaustive Concordance.

INTRODUCTION

I was born in 1953 so I'm what the world refers to as a "baby boomer", a whole generation of people who grew up in the midst of a societal shift which started with most parents who at least vaguely believed that there was a God, but then came World War II and the rise of a pseudo-scientific educational system which strongly taught that our parents were unlearned, superstitious and misinformed about the origins of mankind and the rest of the universe.

World War II left an infected wound in the human race. Many in my parents' generation were spiritually and emotionally messed up and unable to cope adequately after the war. The name PTSD had not even been coined yet, but many people around the world struggled with post-traumatic stress disorder due to the horrors which they had seen and suffered during the war. My parents were no exception, and they tried to deal with life after the war through abuse of alcohol.

I grew up torn between two worlds. I loved my parents when they were sober but I hated them when they were drunk, and they were drunk a lot. I despised conflict and fighting, but every year I got in trouble for fighting at school. I wanted to believe that God exists and that God loves us, but many times during my youth I cursed at God because life seemed so unfair.

I wanted to be a good person, but as my life progressed I found that the evil residing in my own heart destroyed everything that I held dear. I lost my family, my wealth, my reputation, and finally my hope. In the end I saw myself as a complete failure to God and myself and came under such depression and condemnation that I had a strong compulsion to kill myself just to try to end the pain. I was convinced that the world would be better off without me, but God had mercy.

This is the story of how God reached out to me at the crossroads of life and death when I finally realized who my true Father is and how much

He loves me. It's also a wake-up call about a serious sin problem that is running rampant throughout modern Christianity during these end times.

It doesn't matter whether it's dishonesty, monetary crimes, substance abuse, addictions, adultery, premarital sex, child molestation, physical abuse and violence, even murder. There is not any sin that you can name that does not have professing Christians somewhere who are mixed up in it to their eyeballs. All you have to do is listen to the news to understand that the problem extends right up into the highest levels of some Christian leaderships and public ministries.

There are those who believe that God is going to allow this sin-soaked form of Christianity to continue to exist in its present state until Jesus Christ returns to set up His kingdom. They have forgotten the primary reason that God has given us for Christianity's very existence came when Israel was set aside and Christianity was born. They have forgotten that the nation of Israel was cut off from representing God because (even though they were God's chosen people) they too were unrepentant and steeped in sin as a nation, and the day came when Israel was set aside by God and Christianity was born.

I believe that we are now living in the midnight hour before Jesus returns to remove His bride from the Earth. Jesus said the wise will go with Him and the foolish will not. I pray that no professing Christian reading this book will end up in the situation where they are banging on Heaven's closed door after Jesus catches up His Bride only to hear Jesus say "I do not know you. Depart from me evildoers, workers of iniquity. You are appointed to suffer with the unbelievers."

The prophet Hosea declared "My people are destroyed for lack of knowledge". In many churches today, the way to Salvation preached throughout much of Christianity is "another gospel". It is deficient, destroying lives, and many are falling away from Jesus and the way of salvation because of it.

Yet, global Christian revival is still going on right now. More and more people worldwide are accepting that the ministry and gifts of the Holy Spirit are still available to us today. This new wave of Christian revival is being spearheaded by prophets and pastors and priests who once again begin emphasizing the same gospel that Jesus and His disciples preached, the only gospel that will keep God's people on the true path of salvation. The time for the preaching of repentance and solid faith in Jesus Christ is now, before it is too late.

ENDORSEMENTS

I recommend this book to any person who is searching and wants to know what it will take to sell out for Jesus. Michael's personal journey is marked with clear milestones of grace and power through the Holy Spirit who gave him the desire for authentic repentance and surrender to Almighty God. If you are struggling and want to overcome addictions, obsessions and a rebellious heart toward God in your life, then Michael's testimony will encourage you to look to Jesus and His miraculous ability to help you get the victory you want in your life.

Norm Sawyer is a board member and teacher at Kelowna Christian Center.

In an age of so much imitation and falsity I find a genuine and true unfolding of a man's life in this book. So vulnerable, transparent and refreshing with proof that Love does win. A reminder that no one is ever "too far gone."

Dianne Eccles- pastor of Lake Country Life Center

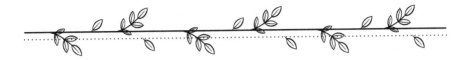

CHAPTER 1

Family History

VICTIMS OF COLLATERAL DAMAGE

The truth is that World War II drastically altered human society. It was not until the late 1930's that the world began to grasp Hitler's end goal for Nazism was total domination of planet Earth. Suddenly young men and teenage boys who were used to learning about life from their parents and their churches were violently thrust into the reality of going off to war to fight and die for God and country. Back at home, their parents and siblings were not much better off.

It was a time in history where children were required to grow up fast. My mother was a Scottish girl of fifteen when Great Britain declared war on Germany in 1939. With no men left to provide an income for the family, she was soon working with her two sisters alongside many other girls and women in the shipbuilding factories of Glasgow. There, Mom labored long hard hours with the other girls and women machining and assembling parts for British battleships and destroyers.

Those were hard times, times of great suffering. Many people wondered if they would still be alive tomorrow. Sometimes they were too mentally, emotionally and physically exhausted to even care anymore. I remember Mom telling me that the German planes would come at night to bomb London and then swing back over Scotland on their return to Germany. Any ordinance remaining was then dumped during their return flights to lighten the load. This would give the German bombers their best chance

1

to make it back home to Germany in one piece. The factories of Glasgow were prime targets.

LIVE FOR TODAY!
TOMORROW YOU COULD DIE.

Mom said that almost every night the air raid sirens would go off and everyone was supposed to make their way to the shelters before the bombs started falling. Often, there was not enough advance warning. Many never made it. Other times, they were so exhausted from their long hours at the factories that they just stayed in bed, choosing that, live or die, they were going to get some sleep that night before they had to go back to the factory the next day.

No one was untouched by the trauma of the war. Fear, shock, pain, guilt, anger, sorrow and remorse are all powerful forces. Not only were the lives of friends and family members lost as soldiers in the war, in our family all of my mom's teeth fell out from shock when she was still a teenager. Mom's older sister's hair also fell out during the war as a result of shock and it never grew back again. Auntie still wears a wig to this day.

By the time the war was finally over, the effect was more or less the same on the world population regardless of whether people had been allies or enemies. This was an entire generation of human beings who began to exhibit signs of post-traumatic stress disorder long before anyone actually identified the syndrome as a bona fide disease. All kinds of physical and emotional problems started to come to the surface in the lives of many people all over the world.

The horrors of what people had seen and experienced during the war coupled with the threat of impending death looming over everyone's head created a moral shift in many people's hearts. Many people developed a determination to "live life to the fullest today because tomorrow you could die". This philosophy fueled by fear became the driving force behind an altered social morality that still thrives in the world today, a morality that comes with its own serious consequences and related problems.

In the years during and after the war, the whole world saw a steady increase in the incidences of premarital and extramarital sex in all its varied forms. Illegitimate births soared. People increasingly turned to psychiatrists and drug dependencies to help deal with their emotional problems (and let's be honest and include smoking, alcohol and prescription pills in the drug category, as well as illegal substances). Family violence and sexual abuse started to become rampant after the war. It turned out that my own family would be no exception.

HAUNTED BY THE TRAUMA OF WAR.
LET'S GET AWAY FROM IT ALL.

Even though their home towns were over five thousand miles apart, my Mom had crossed paths and become intimate with a young Canadian soldier who looked past her toothless grin and wooed her with promises of love and stories of the wide open spaces and peace and prosperity of Canada.

As soon as the war was over, they both decided to do the "right thing" and get married but serious problems began to emerge early in their marriage. Many people do not realize that even today about one in five women will suffer the trauma of a miscarried child during their lifetime. Those numbers rose even more dramatically during the first decade after the World War II.

Mom's first child, a girl, was stillborn, sinking Mom into deep periods of depression. Her husband began turning more and more to alcohol as he battled with his own terrible memories of the war and his inability to help his wife recover from her own depressed condition. Soon a son was born, but the marital dysfunction got worse instead of better. They survived on the hope that once his European military service was over, they could go to Canada and start afresh. However, the truth which many people do not want to accept is that changes in environment cannot permanently cure problems that are not primarily caused by one's environment.

NEW COUNTRY, MORE PROBLEMS

So it was that in 1951 my mother immigrated to Canada with her new husband and young son, but life in Canada was far from the wonderful

3

adventure that had been promised her. Winters can be long and hard in Toronto and it turned out that her husband was not as affluent as he had claimed to be. In fact, he was not well-off at all.

They were relegated to living in a small flat in the low rent district of Toronto. Most of the little money they had left over after bills was being squandered on bouts of drunkenness as her husband tried to cope with the Post Traumatic Stress Disorder that was a result of the things that he had seen and done during the war.

Mom found work at a department store to help make ends meet, but that only led to fights over how the money should be spent. Things started to get more abusive and violent. As a child, I often wondered about Mom's use of heavy makeup throughout most of her life. I eventually found out that it was a habit that she had gotten into as a young woman, not so much to look nice, but to cover the bruises.

If you ever thought that having children will solve marriage problems, I assure you that most of the time it does not work out that way. With extra expenses and bills piling up, things began to get even more verbally abusive and physically violent for Mom at home. Finally, it was too much. Five thousand miles from friends and family and with no one to help her, Mom made a desperate decision. After a particularly brutal physical attack, Mom took her toddler and fled from her husband.

Even back in those days Toronto was a pretty big city and Mom managed to elude her husband for a while. She eventually met another man named Bill who offered to love her and take care of her and her child, but she was far from home free. Trouble was just around the corner.

PRIVATE EYES AND KIDNAPPING

It was like something you read about in a novel, yet this was very real. Mom was unaware that her husband had hired private detectives to hunt her down. They had instructions to find her, then look for an opportunity to grab the baby and return him to his father; and that is exactly what happened.

Thinking that they were now safe, Mom and Bill had left the child with a babysitter while they went to dinner and a movie. While they were gone, a private detective showed up at their residence, bullied his way past the babysitter with bogus legal threats and kidnapped the baby.

Mom was devastated. She went to the Canadian Government for help, but this was the early 1950's. There were no programs to deal with spousal abuse and women's rights. The advice that she got from Social Services was that he was the child's father and "possession was nine-tenths of the law". If she wanted her child, she should go back to her husband where she belonged. She was given this advice in spite of the fact that they were made aware that her husband had threatened by phone to kill her if she ever showed her face again.

Mom told the authorities that she was too afraid of her husband to ever go back to him. As ridiculous as it sounds today, she was then advised that the only other option she had was to look for an opportunity to steal the child back again. They said that once the baby was back in her possession, the Government might then be in a position to help her financially and legally. Mom was too terrified of her husband to try such a thing, and losing her two children was a crushing blow to her.

A HARD CHOICE, A FRESH START, ANOTHER CHILD, WORSE PROBLEMS

Eventually, Bill managed to convince Ella (my Mom) to go west with him in search of a new life and they began working their way toward the west coast. When Ella found out that she was pregnant again, she contacted her husband one last time to ask for a divorce so she could remarry. He coldly refused. So this was the circumstance whereby I was born the illegitimate son of an unfortunate adulterous relationship. My middle name, Barry originates from the coincidence of having the sudden onset of my birth occurring while Mom and Dad were staying at the Barry Hotel in Saskatoon, Saskatchewan on their way west in 1953. Mom never saw her first son again. I know that I have a half-brother somewhere, but I have never been able to locate him.

After my birth, my parents continued their travels westward until settling in the tiny logging community of about 350 residents at Great Central Lake on Vancouver Island. I would like to tell you that things got better from then on, but they did not. My Dad was more than 20 years older than my Mom and in quite poor health.

When she first met him, Mom did not realize that many years of exposure to bright light and inhaling toxic fumes from his trade as a welder was contributing to Bill's bouts of agonizing headaches. This was compounded by uncontrollable fits of rage and paranoia that would only increase over time.

Soon Mom found out that she was again in the same nightmare that she had once escaped from in Toronto. Yes, it was a different face, but the beatings were the same. As for me, I have little memory of my real father other than seeing an angry face accompanied by a hard swung hand coming at me across the kitchen table while Mom did her best to get between us to take the brunt of the beating.

Mercifully, my father died suddenly of a stroke when I was just four years old. They found him in the lake, but the coroner said he was dead before he ever hit the water. It was partly a curse and partly a blessing. Mom was once again free, but now she was a single mother with little income, no one to help her, and local professing Christians were unsympathetic.

RELIGION WITHOUT THE COMPASSION OF CHRIST

I don't want you to get the idea that my parents were total admitted heathens. The war and the after effects of the war contributed a lot to the breaking up of families and to the ungodly behavior that continued after the war throughout most communities. Yet, during the early 1950's most people in Canada still believed in God. However, there were many people in the 1950's walking in various degrees of disobedience to God's Word (just as is still the case today).

Many people from that generation did not really know God the way that God wants us to know Him, nor were they fully following the teachings of Jesus but at least they still practiced some semblance of religion and most residents of small communities still attended church on Sundays.

I don't know what Bill's religious heritage was, but Mom's family was Presbyterian. This meant that, as far as she understood things, she was also a Presbyterian. It was not so much a personal conversion, but a tradition in their family that had been handed down through the generations.

On the other hand, it had not really mattered much to my parents that the one protestant church in Great Central Lake was not Presbyterian. During the few years that they were residents, they attended the only local church there and contributed financially as they were able, like most of the rest of the community. However, things changed when Dad died.

My father's death was my family's first real exposure to formal religion that offered somewhat less than the compassion of Jesus toward hurting people in difficult situations. When Bill died suddenly, Mom got to see the ugly side of religion. You see, this same church owned the only cemetery in the village. They then told a bereaved widow with a four year old child that they could not preside over Bill's funeral or bury him in the cemetery because she had not been legally married to Bill.

They did not want to defile the holy ground of their cemetery by burying a sinner there. Bill and Ella's attendance in church and their contributions to the offering had been welcome in spite of everyone being well aware of their unmarried status, but ironically the church drew the line at allowing his dead body to feed the worms in the cemetery.

In the end, Mom had to pay to have Bill's body shipped out to the closest town with a city-owned cemetery and he was buried in a civil ceremony. It was the first of several bitter experiences that Mom would have with professing Christians over the years, and these would be instrumental in forming a wall between her and salvation through Jesus Christ. It was a wall that would not be broken down until Mom was influenced by the changes that God was making in my own life, and those changes would not happen until many years later when she was nearly sixty years old.

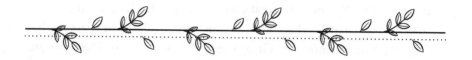

CHAPTER 2

Alcoholism and Addictions

I GET A NEW FATHER

Mom couldn't bear to stay at Great Central Lake after that experience so she settled in the larger nearby town of Alberni where she met a widower named Norm. They hit it off, and we all moved to Duncan a short time afterward. Norm owned a small two bedroom house in that town, and he had been renting out to an older lady. When she passed away, we all moved in. I remember my bedroom was so small that my parents decided to set up my bed in the closet to give me a little more space to play in the room.

My step-dad Norm was generally a decent guy. He was a good worker, well liked in the community and I believe that he genuinely loved me and my mother. Even though we were not wealthy, Norm tried to be a good provider. I always had food, clothes and a roof over my head as a child, but there were other problems in Norm and Ella's lives, real serious problems.

Norm was also an ex-serviceman and had never really gotten over losing his first wife at a young age. It was hard on him. Unfortunately Norm tried to block out those memories by drinking, and he drank a lot. He regularly drank himself into oblivion to try to cope with having lost his first wife at such a young age. Plus, it was not helping that he now had to deal with a new spouse who had her own battles with depression as a result of losing two children and two husbands. Soon the fighting began in earnest.

Mom had never been much of a drinker up to this point, but she began to accept the philosophy of "if you can't beat them, join them" and it was not long before they both had a full blown alcohol problem. As for me, I was quickly becoming an emotional wreck before I even hit puberty.

CHILDREN, THE HIDDEN VICTIMS OF ALCOHOL AND DRUGS

One thing that the use of alcohol and drugs does is that it dulls one's senses and warps reality, often making the participants completely oblivious to the effect that their deviant behavior is having on family and friends. In case you did not realize it, let me explain to you that a closed door to a child's room does not drown out the sounds of parents who curse and swear and violently fight like cats and dogs, repeatedly threatening to leave and split up the family. Your children hear what is going on behind the closed doors and it is terrifying them, traumatizing them.

There were many days during Elementary School when I was so burdened by what was going on at home that I literally could not get to sleep until the fighting stopped. Sometimes that was not until one parent or the other returned in the early hours of the morning after storming out in the middle of the night, threatening to never come back. In my early years, I was frightened, hurting and lost a lot of sleep.

Sometimes I blamed myself when they were fighting, especially if I had misbehaved. As I grew older, those feelings of fear turned to anger, resentment and rebellion. I rarely brought friends over to avoid the risk of embarrassment that occurred when my falling down drunk parents tried to interact with them. Bringing a girl home was simply unthinkable.

During my teens I actually wasn't much of a troublemaker. I really wanted to be a good person, but if anyone tried to bully me, watch out. I would take all the rage and resentment that I felt toward my parents and vent my anger upon the person who thought that the skinny new kid would be an easy target. I never showed them much mercy. As far as I was concerned, they were at fault for attacking me and now they were going to pay for the suffering I was enduring at home. I couldn't strike back at my parents, but I could certainly hurt the bullies. I didn't hold back if they pushed me too far.

I actually hated fighting. I never started a fight. I wanted a peaceful existence, but the bullies seemed to think that this was a sign of weakness. Every year for the first ten years of school I got the strap for fighting. In those days, corporal punishment still existed in the schools and it did not matter who started the fight. You both got the strap. It hardly seemed fair to me at the time, the same punishment for the aggressors and their targets, but that's the way it was.

PORNOGRAPHY, THE ADDICTION
NO ONE WANTS TO TALK ABOUT

I was only eight years old when my best buddy who lived next door showed me a magazine with explicit sexual content that his older brother had smuggled in from the United States and the images and the sensations that they produced immediately changed my life. That one exposure to pornography was an emotional and spiritual seed that would quickly grow into an addiction to pornography that would last for decades and eventually contribute to the destruction of my own marriage.

The initial appeal to pornography is that it is pleasing and arousing to look at, but many people do not realize that there is a demonic hook to pornography. The release of emotional and sexual tensions which are associated with the use of porn are addictive and totally self-serving.

I soon found out that pornography and the activity that it stimulates gave me the emotional release and relaxation that I needed to get to sleep even when my parents were in the midst of an all-out war in the next room. Mom wasn't thrilled about finding porn in my room but Dad convinced her that this was just something that boys do and there was no real harm in it.

I did not even realize what was happening at first, but soon something that had started out as an exciting curiosity gradually grew into an addictive practice. Before long, I was not able to get to sleep without pornography and the emotional and sexual release that comes with it. Furthermore, as is the case with many emotional and physical addictions, familiarity lessens the effect of pornography. You are always on the hunt for a new and better high, always looking for something more explicit and more arousing wherever you can find it.

PORNOGRAPHY, NOT A VICTIMLESS CRIME!

It's a tragedy that pornography is a forbidden topic in Christian circles because the sad truth is that many professing Christians struggle with an addiction to pornography today. The internet now makes it so easy to keep porn addiction hidden from others within the darkness of people's own homes, but Satan also endeavors to silence our consciences by arguing that pornography is harmless diversion, a victimless crime. Yet pornography is not victimless and not harmless, no not at all. Its destructiveness is far-reaching.

Porn changes the way that people view and think about other people. It prematurely draws young children into the realm of sexuality long before they are emotionally mature enough to manage lustful desires. Pornography is also totally self-centered. Instead of stimulating your interest in other human beings as people, you become less interested in people as God's children and more fixated on what they might look like naked, in trying to see them naked. Your only goal becomes how they can satisfy your sexual needs.

Is pornography victimless? Tell that to some of the young children who have managed to get their hands on pornography and become so overstimulated that they go to the next step of molesting their siblings or peers. Also, don't delude yourself about this next fact. If you have pornography in your home, your children **will** find it and it will influence their thinking toward evil and ungodliness.

Since becoming a minister, I have counselled many people in and from the prison system. There are a huge number of men and woman in jail right now for sexual crimes who will admit to you that pornography was present in their formative childhood years and it played a part in the development of their abnormal sexual appetites and sexual crimes.

Porn addiction is no excuse for sexual crime. Porn addiction does not absolve anyone of their guilt or responsibility for sin. What porn does do is influence some people toward sexual addiction and deviance in the same manner that booze and drugs influences some people toward addiction to those substances and the sinful behavior that follows.

Do you think pornography is harmless? Talk to the teens and single adults who find it almost impossible to relate to the opposite sex in a decent way because pornography is fueling their lust to the point where their primary goal in life has become trying to get someone else naked and have sex with them. They don't really care about other people. They just care about satisfying their compulsion for sexual release.

If you think that pornography is not harmful, talk to the married men and women who have become so addicted and self-centered because of pornography and marital aids that they would rather relieve themselves artificially because it is quicker and easier than taking the time and making the effort to satisfy their spouse. Their spouse no longer arouses them anymore to the same degree that the porn does.

What about the porn itself? Are you deceived into thinking this humongous quantity of pictures and videos were all taken voluntarily? Talk to the children and men and women who are used and abused by the criminal element of society to produce pornography. Many are forced to do what they do. Some do so because it is the only way they know how to make enough money to support their drug addictions. Others are so emotionally and spiritually damaged that they do not believe that they deserve a better life than to be used and abused by other greedy and demented people in the making of porn.

Pornography is not a victimless crime! It is the gateway to abuse, emotional instability, spiritual damage, bodily injury and disease, even to physical abuse and death. Stop deceiving yourself. Porn is of sin and Satan, not of God.

Godly sexuality is always love-centered and spouse-centered. Pornography and all other forms of sexual immorality are always self-centered, sin-centered and demon-influenced. Pornography is one of the most insidious tools that Satan has at his disposal to try to prevent and pervert the love and beauty that God intended to occur only between a husband and wife for as long as they both shall live.

People think it can't be all that bad, but I tell you that it is. As far as a psychologically destructive substance, porn is every bit as addictive as cigarettes, alcohol, cocaine or heroin to a large portion of society. I soon found out that once you realize that you are hooked and you try to stop, porn addicts experience the same tremors, emotional stress and sleeplessness that any other addicts suffer. If they can't trade it or buy it, severe porn addicts will even stoop to stealing it or raking through the trash to get it. That's how bad it is, for some people, and I was no exception.

There is an evil spirit behind pornography and it is one that is dedicated to destroying lives and families. Regardless of the addiction, all addictions have demonic spiritual roots. All addictions are demonically engineered to be destroyers of families in some manner. They destroy physical and emotional health. They destroy relationships, they can destroy reputations, and they contribute to crime.

In the beginning porn seemed to be a harmless way to help in dealing with the many problems of adolescence. I did not realize it at the time, but even as an elementary school child I was headed down the road to being bound by porn, which was only one of numerous other addictions which would all eventually become instrumental in destroying my life, my family, my reputation and my credibility as a Christian.

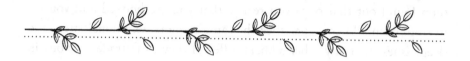

CHAPTER 3

I Don't Fit Anywhere

GEEKS, PRUDES, JOCKS and HOODS

Anyone who has ever been to high school is probably familiar with these clique terms but in case you are not, I'll fill you in. When I went to school, if you were smart you were a geek. If you were religious, you were a prude. If you were athletic, you were a jock and if you were overly ill-behaved, you were a hood. There were also the druggies who were mostly composed of hoods, but often included members from the other groups as well.

Lastly, there was one more group, the one that I fit into, if you could call it fitting in. These were the loners a.k.a. the weirdos. I was usually one of the new kids in school because my step-dad had a habit of losing jobs due to his alcohol problem. Then we would have to move to another town, another school and start life all over again.

I was smart enough to be a geek, but not willing to put in the effort to get the grades. In fact, ten years after dropping out of high school, I finished my grade 12 through the GED program with a ninety-six percentile average. Then I successfully completed a MENSA exam. Yet the achievement was not important enough to me for me to send MENSA the money they wanted to acknowledge me as a card-carrying member. Let's face it. I'm Scottish so I was reluctant to part with a substantial amount of money for a piece of paper just to promote my own vanity. Yet I was still proud that I did well.

Neither did I fit in with the prudes. Even though Mom had taught me her vague concepts about God, Jesus, Heaven and Hell, I had trouble reconciling those teachings with my porn addiction and what we were being taught in school about evolution. I hadn't made up my mind about evolution yet and my behavior tended to lean more toward that of the hoods than the prudes anyway. So, I wasn't interested in spending a lot of time with religious fanatics (as the prudes were also called), so that kept me out of their social circles.

I was actually athletic enough to win ribbons and medals but rarely motivated to put in the effort and commitment to make it happen. Sometimes a teacher would convince me to reluctantly go win a ribbon or two for the school if some team member failed to show up on sports day.

I don't know if they still do it at schools today, but back then one of the events on sports day at school was the "ball throw". It worked somewhat like shotput in that the contestants would all stand at home plate on the baseball field and throw a softball as far as they could. Then someone in the outfield would mark where the ball first hits the ground and the people who threw the ball the farthest would win ribbons for first, second and third.

I never entered the contest, but I would sometimes pick up a ball that had landed and rolled a good distance farther. Then I somewhat enjoyed firing it back full force against the backstop far above everybody's heads just to let them know that I could win if I really wanted to, but I couldn't be bothered. I much preferred to be out hiking, fishing, hunting, riding motorcycles or getting drunk or stoned.

Truly, the group that I identified with the most was the hoods. They respected me because of my ability to fight, although I wasn't mean enough (or dumb enough) to want to become part of their inner circle. The reality was that I didn't really fit in anywhere. I never had many close friends growing up because I was always an outsider. At each new school I would end up trying to avoid the bullies for as long as possible while bonding with one or two of the other weirdos who shared some of the same common interests I had.

GIRLS, SEX & PORN

I am certainly not very proud to admit that this was pretty well the whole life focus of my activities during my teen and early adult years, but that's the way it was. My search for a sexual partner proved to be a big dilemma for me. When I was younger, my parents and the Bible both taught me that that I should abstain from sex until I got married.

Later on, the focus of my parents' advice shifted toward assuming that I was going to have sex before marriage (because that's what they had done) and educating me about safe sex to make sure that I didn't get someone pregnant. Of course, that conflict of values didn't do much to help me with my own inner moral struggles I was going through regarding right and wrong.

I wasn't looking for meaningless sexual encounters. I was a lonely young man looking for a life-long commitment, someone to share my life with. I wanted to love and be loved in a way that my own parents didn't seem to be capable of, but this put me in conflict with my porn fueled adolescent sex urges that were constantly driving me to try to get to the sex part long before I was interested in the marriage part.

My situation was not helped by the fact that I grew up in the abundant "dope" and "free love" era of late sixties and seventies when birth control pills were becoming readily available to teens and Biblical morality was waning. It was starting to be "the thing to do" for people to get high and try out sex to make sure that you were compatible before actually committing to marriage, and the ungodly were beginning to demand that the church stay out of the "bedrooms" of society

I am not going to give the devil any glory by going into the details. Suffice it to say that it did not take me long to learn that irrational decisions made while you are high on drugs and/or alcohol combined with uncommitted loveless sex does nothing to bring fulfilment into your life. I never gave up looking for the right person to spend the rest of my life with but porn continued to deeply influence my sexual appetites, relationships and ungodly behavior throughout my teens and early adult years.

MOTORCYCLES, CARS, AND GUNS

When I wasn't thinking about sex, I loved the sense of the open air, the freedom, and a certain amount of fearful respect that comes with a black leather jacket and riding a loud and powerful motorcycle. I was never part of a gang. I didn't want to be. I didn't like the idea of being vulnerable or answerable to anybody.

The same outlaw thinking carried over to my cars and trucks as well. I was the guy with the 454 cubic inch Chevelle convertible and the small box pickup with the Firebird 400 engine and transmission shoe-horned into it and my few friends also had similar vehicles. We would make a game out of roaring around town on weekends at high speeds until the cops were looking for us and then we would just switch vehicles and do it all over again, partly ignorant, and partly uncaring about the danger we were to ourselves and to the rest of society.

As far as guns go, I had a lot of them. I bought more than a few unregistered weapons from the back of someone's vehicle when I was still a teenager and always owned at least a few weapons. I even built my own working forty caliber flintlock pistol. Gun laws were more lax back then. It was still illegal to carry a pistol on your person back then, yet I did, and I knew quite a few other people who did.

Even before the movie "Dirty Harry" came out, it was not at all unusual for me and my buddies to go out riding or just walking around town with a six inch hunting knife hanging on our belt and a magnum pistol tucked inside our belt hidden under our shirts just in case we needed it. We were never looking for violence but I was determined not to be a victim, so I was always prepared and capable of dealing with trouble if trouble came looking for me.

I was an expert marksman with a pistol, rifle and bow. I could reliably shoot pennies stuck in a fence post from a distance of 20 yards and earned a silver medal in the Canadian Archery championships when I was still in my teens. This included hitting targets up to one hundred yards away with a bow and arrow. As the new kid in school, I would inevitably be tested by one of the local bullies.

In my later teens and as a young adult it never took very long for word to get around that this guy was an armed biker with a violent temper when provoked. Usually one fight was all it took and the bullies found someone else to harass.

The bad guys didn't like me much, but it was never my intention to be part of their scene anyway. The motorcycle, the guns and the violent reputation existed to send out a clear message that this was not someone that you should be messing with. Just leave me alone. When someone didn't take the hint, a crazed look and some violently aggressive language was usually all it took to get them to back down. Even as a child, on the rare occasions that this was not enough of a deterrent, I would go after the attacker with such a vicious rage that it would frighten those who witnessed it and the bully would never make the same mistake again.

Sometimes, I really wanted to kill the guy. I wanted to make him pay for all of the injustices that I had suffered growing up, but somehow I always managed to stop short of using deadly force on anybody. It was like there was one voice in my head that was telling me to go ahead, while another voice that I now know was the voice of God was saying "Don't do it"! Deep down, I really didn't want to hurt anyone. I was just determined that I was not going to be hurt anymore myself.

GETTING DRUNK AND
GETTING HIGH

Some people think that growing up in small town Canada would be pretty lame and tame, but that all depended upon how you were raised and who you knew. For the devoutly religious crowd and the law-abiding citizens, life was pretty quiet, but we were the kids who were stealing booze from the fridge in our early teens while our parents partied it up in another room too wasted to know what was going on.

This was also back in the days when bar owners were not very careful about checking ID's. Even though the legal drinking age was twenty-one and I looked older than I was when I was a teenager, I'm sure that many bartenders knew that we were under age, yet I was getting into bars when I was sixteen. As long as we didn't cause any trouble, we were rarely refused entrance or asked to leave. When it came to alcohol and drugs though, the real action was not at the bars. It was at the private parties around town.

In smaller towns, most people are at least casually acquainted with others who run in similar circles. In pretty well any small town that I was ever in (if you knew where to go) all you had to do was show up at a known party house with some dope or a bag of booze. You were usually welcomed in to spend the rest of the night whooping it up with whoever happened to be there. Pity the poor property owners the next day. Sometimes the damage was pretty extensive.

There was one thing that I did avoid, however. I stayed away from the highly addictive illegal drugs. I was not so much against them from a moral standpoint, but I had seen far too many people in my life turned into walking zombies because of these drugs and did not want to end up in the same condition. Nonetheless, there were still more than a few occasions where I got so wasted on booze and/or drugs that I would pass out completely, close to alcohol poisoning I am sure.

I once woke up in the rafters of a barn with no idea of how I got there. On another occasion I called a friend to come and get me because I was too drunk to stand up, let alone drive home. He found me passed out in the snow underneath my truck in below zero weather. Some would say that I was lucky to still be alive. I believe that it was God who continued to spare me from certain death over and over again so that I would be able to use this book to warn others and teach others about God's longsuffering love and forgiveness toward man, including you and me, dear reader.

If you think that any of the things that I have told you about my life are more interesting or exciting than the life you might have led, you need to get those ideas out of your head right now. I am deeply ashamed of the life that I led as a young man and if I could do it all over again, I would want to have served God with all my heart right from the day that I was born.

My years of sin and rebellion were a continuous source of pain and heartache for me and I came close to death so many times as a teen and a young man that I realize now that it was only by the grace of God that I survived all those years without becoming crippled or killed. I know beyond the shadow of any doubt that I am here today only by the love and mercy of God.

I am telling you my story in the hope that it will help some readers realize the foolishness of the life that I led and not make the same mistakes that I made. This book was also written to give hope to those who are already caught in the same or similar traps as the ones that destroyed my life. I don't ever want you to go the way I went, but I am also telling you my story to help people understand that it doesn't matter what you have done in the past, you can still change your life now. You are not beyond saving if you really want to come to God. The Lord does love you and He can and will help you if you make the decision to repent (turn away) from your past evils and come back to God, accepting Him as your true father.

DON'T USE CHRISTIANS
TO JUDGE CHRISTIANITY

One of the things that you will need to learn in this life is that sometimes you are going to run into people who call themselves Christians, yet their lives are still full of sin. They do not accept or have not been taught that repentance (turning away from all evil) is an integral and essential part of God's message of Salvation for the human race through Jesus Christ. Please don't let their error deter you from coming to God. Yes, their behavior is evil but they are like rebellious children and in many cases, they don't know any better because they have been misled by leaders who are wolves in sheep's clothing.

Their ungodly behavior does not mean that the Bible is not true, or that God does not care about us, or that Jesus is not our Savior. It only means that these people are unlearned, disobedient and in need of repentance. They have never been properly taught the way of salvation. Such sinful human behavior and their warped beliefs are the product of the evil and corrupt seeds that have been sown in their lives. It does not change the fact that God loves you deeply. I'm telling every person reading this that the Word of God is still all-powerful and well able to redeem every person who come to Jesus Christ for mercy, forgiveness and Salvation and this includes you and me.

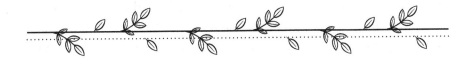

CHAPTER 4

Professing Christians

MY EARLY YEARS AND RELIGION

I already told you the story about the local church that banned my dad's dead body from their graveyard, but there are a few other memorable things that happened during my childhood that turned my family away from Christianity.

The first incident involved the large piece of property and small two bedroom house that my step-dad owned. It was okay for Norm when he was single but really too small to be comfortable for us as a family. Dad put the house and large lot up for sale and we moved into a bigger house on the other side of town. After a while Dad received a call from a couple who asked if they could take a look at the house.

Norm agreed to meet them at the house and was greeted by a pleasant couple who maintained that they had just recently immigrated to Canada and were looking for an affordable place to purchase for their retirement. They told him that this was just what they had been looking for but they did not have a lot of money. They asked if Dad could help them out by giving them a substantial discount off his asking price.

Now, Norm may have had his faults but he also had a tender heart and soft spot for people. Even though our family needed the money and their offer was considerably lower than he wanted to go, he sold them the property at the reduced price to help them out.

A few months later, we happened to be on that side of town so Dad decided to drive by the house to see how the couple was doing. What he found was that the house and gardens were gone and there was a large brand new church on the property. Whoever was behind it all must have started building the thing right after they bought the property. Needless to say, Dad had more than a few descriptive things to say about that church and they weren't very complimentary.

The next negative experiences with people who claimed to be Christians came in the form of renters. The first was a family who were renting a trailer that Dad owned. After a couple of missed rent payments, Dad stopped by to see what was going on. What he found was that these professing Christians had not only skipped town, they had taken the trailer with them, never to be seen again, and dad had no insurance.

Later on he rented out another house to a couple who were supposed to be Christians. They did so much damage to the house and property before skipping out owing three month's rent that Dad had to sell everything at a loss because he could not afford to make the thousands of dollars in repairs that were necessary to fix the house up again.

As with many would be-Christians, Mom and Dad liked the idea of God and Jesus and Christianity, but they had been burned so many times by professing Christians that they eventually got to the place where they stopped attending church and did not want to have much to do anymore with those who called themselves Christians. How sad is this.

SUNDAY SCHOOL AND BOY SCOUTS

When you consider some of their bad experiences with people who had called themselves Christians, I was surprised when my parents did let me go off to Sunday school with one the neighborhood kids when I was invited, but they never went to church themselves unless it was a Christmas or Easter pageant that I was part of.

Mom and Dad also considered the Cub and Boy Scouts to be somewhat of a Christian based wholesome organization, so when one of my friends encouraged me to join, my parents supported my desire to go with my friend. I enjoyed Sunday school and the Cubs and Scouts when I was younger, but eventually quit everything after one too many ordeals of being left in the dark cursing and crying on the steps of the scouting hall long after everyone else had gone home.

You see, Mom and Dad developed the habit of going to the bar while I was at Cubs, and later Scouts. Then they would lose track of time. Finally (sometimes hours later) they would show up absolutely bombed to drive me home. I remember one instance when Dad drove off the road into the ditch until he hit a culvert that diverted him back onto the road again. He was so plastered that he didn't even realize what had happened. Then this was usually followed by them fighting all night about the whole thing while I was trying to get to sleep.

Eventually I did not want to deal with it anymore. First I quit Sunday school, then Scouts. Parents have no idea of the trauma and confusion that it puts their children through when they tell their children that God and Jesus loves us in the daytime and then spend several nights a week after the sun goes down cursing and swearing at each other, physically abusing one another, threatening to kill each other, or threatening to leave the family and never come back.

READING THE BIBLE AND RANTING AT GOD

In my later teens, Mom gave me her cherished copy of the King James Bible after Norm threatened to tear it up in a drunken rage. Sometimes I would read it, wondering if the stories were actually true. Some parts were boring, but other parts were quite interesting to me, particularly the parts about Jesus Christ, who was not much like any of the Christians that I had ever met.

Sometimes when I was going through a particularly rough time at home, I would pray, hoping that there was a God somewhere up there who cared enough to be listening and willing to do something about my family. Other times, I would stomp out into the woods until I found a secluded place where I would curse and swear at God. I would shake my fist in the air, waving it at God, ranting about my problems for extended periods and challenging God to reveal Himself to me if He wanted me to believe in Him.

I never heard God say anything during these temper tantrums, but strangely enough they calmed me down and I would come away feeling better. It was as if God had somehow heard and understood my frustrations even if He was not going to answer me directly, or immediately do anything about my messed up family situation.

1972 – DEATH COMES KNOCKING

I was 19 years old, returning home to a job offer after being on my own away from Mom and Dad since I was seventeen. I had just bought a souped up Chevelle two weeks previously and was pushing it to the limit on the way home. As I neared the town of Quesnel about five hundred miles into a seven hundred mile trip, I had the car almost flying, averaging over a hundred miles an hour and passing cars like they were standing still whenever the traffic allowed.

I soared over the crest of a hill coming down into the town of Quesnel and grew immediately angry because I could see that I was going to have to slow down due to the heavy traffic. I had to drop my speed to about fifty miles per hour and was blocked in by traffic on all sides when suddenly it happened. Someone in a three quarter ton truck waiting to turn left across the highway was momentarily blinded by the sun setting behind my vehicle. They did not see my car and turned head on right into me. It was all over before I even had time to move my foot from the gas pedal to the brake pedal.

My car careened off their truck into a steel lamppost and all of my belongings that had been stacked in the back of the car came pouring over the seat helping to pin me in the driver's compartment. Passersby quickly came and helped extricate me from the vehicle. The police and ambulance must have also been close by as well because they were there almost immediately and began administering first aid.

The policeman checked me over, then asked me to sit on the curb and wait for him to help the ambulance attendants provide medical assistance to the other people involved in the crash. The people in the other vehicle were quite seriously injured and would need to be taken to the hospital right away. He explained to me that when he was finished, he would return to take me to the hospital as well. I sat on the curb for a while and then tried to stand, but every time I tried to stand up to see what was going on, I got dizzy and had to sit down again.

Finally, the policeman returned and offered to help me into his car for the trip to the hospital. At first I protested a little, saying that I was just a little dizzy and didn't think that I needed to go to a hospital. Then the policeman told me that I was bleeding and he pointed to my chest. When I looked down to see my chest covered in blood, I realized that the reason that I was dizzy was that I had split my chin wide open and had suffered a pretty serious concussion. Later on at the hospital they stitched me up and kept me overnight for observation. Then I was given a clean bill of health and told that I was OK to go. I didn't think too much about the whole thing. I never comprehended how serious the accident really was until I went back to retrieve my belongings from my car the next day.

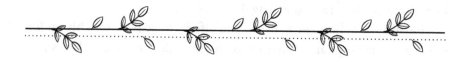

CHAPTER 5

Did I Hear?

EXAMINING THE WRECKAGE

The day following the accident I talked with the police and the insurance company. They assured me that there were plenty of witnesses who testified that the other driver was at fault and their insurance was going to cover all of my costs including a replacement vehicle and any lost time off work. That was a relief.

Later on I went to the wreckers to retrieve my belongings from the car. Then and only then did it begin to dawn on me how close to death I had actually come. The people in the other vehicle had suffered broken limbs, broken ribs and smashed faces. Yet aside from six stitches in my chin and a little soreness in my thumbs I had come through the accident relatively unscathed even though I had not been wearing a seatbelt.

Consequently, I was pretty unnerved when I took my first look at the car. The headlights were just outside of the broken windshield, the motor was humped up through the floor and both doors were buckled so badly that they wouldn't even come close to closing. The only things salvageable were the new rear tires that I had just bought.

Then I saw the steering wheel and understood why my thumbs were sore. I had bent the steering wheel completely in half. It was then that I realized that (since I had not been wearing a seatbelt) if either my thumbs or the steering wheel had broken, my chest would have undoubtedly been crushed by the steering column or I could have gone through the windshield.

The most disturbing thought came to me when I remembered that less than 60 seconds before the accident I had been travelling at over one hundred miles an hour. It was very obvious to me that if I had hit their vehicle at that speed, everyone involved would have almost certainly been killed.

That's when I heard the voice.

GOD DOES SPEAK TO US.

As I was thinking about the events that had just transpired and how close I had come to dying, I clearly heard someone say to me "If not for me, you would be dead." It was so clear that I turned my head to see who was talking to me, but there was no one there. It was then that I realized that I had not heard the voice with my ears, but with my spirit, and at that moment in my life, God suddenly became real to me.

I know that there are those who would suggest that I just imagined hearing a voice or that I only heard it because I wanted to hear it. Yet I was not at all a particularly religious person at that point in my life. I was not even thinking about God at the time. I was only there to get my stuff and contemplating how close I had come to death.

I assure you, I know what I heard and it instantly changed my life. It started me on a nine year journey of trying to understand and learn everything I could about this God who had spoken to me and claimed to have kept me from dying. If God was real, then I wanted to learn more about Him.

CHOOSING A RELIGION

For once in my life I now had a goal and a purpose, I wanted to find out about God. That was the day that clinched things for me in the argument between Atheism and belief in God. For me, ever since 1972 the score has been God 1-Atheism 0. God wins, but I still had a lot to learn.

The next big challenge was for me to decide which religion (if any of them) was closest to what I believed to be the truth.

Obviously, Atheism as a religion was no longer a viable argument to me, but what about all the other religions in the world? They all disagreed with one another so they could not all be right. Were any of them right? I wanted to find out.

Now don't get me wrong. Even though I knew deep within my being that God had spoken to me, this does not mean that I turned into a religious fanatic overnight. My experience never really changed my lifestyle or behavior patterns. The only change in my life at that point was that I was now intensely interested in learning more about God.

I am a realist. I am an open minded person. I didn't start with any agenda to promote any particular religion, and from past experiences, traditional Christianity was certainly not at the top of my list. You could say that I was at the time a sincere seeker, unconverted, but extremely curious to learn more about God. I studied all of the major religions in detail and a lot of the more obscure ones as well. After four years of intense study I came to the intellectual decision that Christianity was indeed probably the most believable of all the religions that I had examined.

This was actually not an easy conclusion for me come to. I was impressed by the general message of the Bible, particularly the New Testament and the teachings of Jesus, but a lot of it was confusing to me. Plus, I was thoroughly disillusioned and disappointed with the behavior of most of the people that I had met throughout my life who had claimed to be Christians. God, I liked. Christians, not so much.

With their mouths they said they were Christians, but their attitudes, language and behavior were really no better than mine, and in some cases, it was atrocious. I considered many of them to be worse people than I was. So I stayed away from churches and tried to figure out Christianity on my own. It was not the wisest decision I ever made. Really, I was trying to create my own version of Christianity, hoping that I could make it work for me and still keep my own sinful lifestyle.

UNINSPIRED RELIGION PLUS
BAD BEHAVIOR PRODUCES
DEFECTIVE DISCIPLES

Like many people, I was drawn to Jesus and Christianity. It was just people who professed to be Christians that I did not have much use for because their behavior did not line up with what came out of their mouths. It bothered me that there was not any sin that you could name that there was not someone somewhere claiming to be Christian that was mixed up in it right up to the eyeballs.

At that point in my life (through my job) I was often responsible for training new employees. I would cringe inside whenever someone new would tell me right away that they were a Christian because in the end it would often turn out that they were lousy workers. Sometimes they would turn out to be real theological fruit loops as well. Their beliefs often turned out to be far from what the Bible actually teaches. There was one woman at work who was a professing Christian and thought that there was nothing wrong with topless sunbathing in public. Anyone who disagreed with her was accused of having a dirty mind.

This proved to be a real stumbling block for me in my own search for Salvation. On the one hand, I knew that such behavior testified that these people were not right with God. On the other hand, I tended to use their behavior as a balance scale to justify the continuing sins that were still going on in my own life, like the blind leading the blind.

I deceived myself into thinking that if these sinners were going to make it into Heaven, God certainly wasn't going to keep me out. It didn't really occur to me at the time that (according to God's Word) none of us would make it because the Bible declares that no evildoers will be going with Jesus when He comes for His Bride. They were just as far from God as I was. We were actually all deceived workers of iniquity and still following our father Satan.

I WAS NOT A CHRISTIAN.
I ONLY THOUGHT I WAS.

At that time in my life, I could certainly tell you what the Bible said or did not say. I had read it through numerous times in several different translations. However, I now understand that knowing about God and knowing what God says is not the same as trusting God, believing God and being obedient to God. It is one thing to acknowledge that God exists, but that is not at all the same as being willing to trust and obey Him as our Father in Heaven. It is not the same as developing an intimate, personal and obedient relationship with God.

Just to give you an idea of how mixed up my concept of Christianity was, let me tell you this story. In the mid-seventies I was still a young man in my early twenties and I was lonely for a female companion. I wasn't out looking for hookers or one-night stands. I was looking for a woman to love, marry and have as my wife for the rest of my life. I even prayed to God with tears, promising God that if He brought me a wife, I would serve Him for the rest of my life.

Now, that might seem like a sincere prayer to a lot of people, but after praying such prayers, I would then go out into the bars and the cabarets and the party houses at night looking for someone who was interested in becoming my wife.

They went out of business years ago, but one of the more popular bars that I used to frequent was originally called "The Devil's Web Cabaret". I grasp now how creepy and ironic that this was, but at the time I didn't see the connection or the contradiction between what I was praying for and the way I was living. I was blinded by my own sinful behavior. Later on, I would learn that the Word of God has a lot to say about the way that I was behaving at that point in my life:

> He that turns away his ear from hearing the law, even his prayer shall be abomination.
> Proverbs 28:9 KJV

> God has no use for the prayers of the people who won't listen to him Proverbs 28:9 MSG

A RELIGIOUS "CONVERSION"
BUILT UPON DECEPTION

The Bible explains to us that one of the greatest obstacles interfering with people reaching a true salvation experience with God is the fact that our own human nature is corrupted. We have been corrupted by evil to such an extent that our own hearts become deceived by our wickedness. Our own sinfulness will influence us to omit or twist any parts of the Word of God that contradict our evil behavior. We place an over-emphasis on Scriptures which may appear on the surface to excuse or support continuing evil behavior in our lives, but are blind to the rest of God's Word.

> The heart is deceitful above all things, and desperately wicked: who can know it?
> Jeremiah 17:9 KJV

> There is a way that seems right to a man, but its end is the way of death. Proverbs 16:25 NKJV

> There's a way that looks harmless enough; look again - it leads straight to hell. Proverbs 16:25 MSG

That's why it didn't bother me when I met someone back then at the Devil's Web Cabaret who also professed to be a Christian. We were attracted to one another and eventually made a commitment to love one another. It did not seem wrong back then for me to move in with someone who already had two children and was separated but still married to someone else. We rationalized it away by pointing out that God is a God of love and the only thing that was important to us was that we loved each other.

In our own minds, we had deceived ourselves into thinking that Christianity was all about philosophical love, and love trumped everything. I convinced myself that because her husband had sinned against his family he deserved to be rejected. I thought that I was justified in taking over where he had failed. Yet from the very beginning, deception was deeply woven into our relationship.

We did not want to be perceived as living in sin so we lied to our church, our friends and my parents, telling them all that we had eloped and gotten married in another town. Yes, that bothered me, but we felt that we loved one another and it was a white lie that would disappear on its own as soon as we could legally get married.

It also bothered me considerably when her husband would show up to see his kids and I could see the love in his eyes that he still had for his children. Then it really bothered me when he later on committed suicide. I felt partially responsible, but I rationalized it away with the argument that I really loved this woman and her children. In my mind, I saw it as somewhat of a parallel to what had happened with my own mother and father and how they had come together.

When her first husband committed suicide I even convinced myself that God had taken this man out of the way so that we could get married. The truth is that I was walking and repeating the same sinful path that my own parents had taken. Later on in life, I would learn a hard lesson about what the Word of God means when it says that when it comes to sin, we reap what we sow in this life.

CHAPTER 6

True Christians?

TRYING TO BE CHRISTIAN WITHOUT
FIRST SUBMITTING TO JESUS CHRIST

My partner and I bought wedding rings to further the charade that we were married and went together up to the altar at a local church and proclaimed that we believed in Jesus Christ as our Savior. Then we were both baptized shortly afterward in one of the local lakes and started attending church regularly.

After my partner's husband died in 1976, we were able to actually get married and a short time later my son was born. We started several successful businesses and quickly became recognized as pillars of the church and the community. We even sold Bibles and Christian literature through a retail business that we owned.

We witnessed to others about God, Jesus, Christianity and Salvation. In our minds we were just as much Christians as anyone else who said they were a Christian. For a short while, it seemed as though we would live happily ever after and then go to be with Jesus, but then things started to fall apart.

We made some unwise business decisions that soon left us with a huge debt load. Then both the lumber and mining industries began to sag. Our town was built on these industries and suddenly many people were laid off and not spending anymore. Many businesses (including ours) were in deep trouble. I could see that our businesses were fast headed for bankruptcy but instead of turning to God, I pulled away from God and away from my wife. I returned once again to alcohol, drugs and pornography to try to deal with the stresses and the emotional instability in my life.

What I did not realize was that turning away from God and back to sin never solves anyone's problems. It only deadens our own consciousness of their presence for a short time. In the process, it actually makes all of your problems worse. The more we sin, the more out of touch with reality and the more self-centered we become in our behavior.

I began to fall into fits of rage and frustration toward my wife and children, just as my own father had done, but the greatest contributor to the destruction of my family was pornography. Contrary to what many believe, pornography is not a marital aid. Yes, it inflames your sexual desires, but it does not inflame your desire for your spouse. Pornography is completely self-centered. Porn can become so addictive that it increases your desire for sex with anyone, as long as it satisfies the lust. The end result was that porn fueled my sexual desires until my sexual sin destroyed my marriage and spiritually and emotionally crushed my wife and children

At first I tried to blame God. Why had God allowed this to happen to me? But God did not do this. I did. Jesus has this to say about the religion of those who are unrepentant. It doesn't matter what our religion is, Christian or otherwise:

> "What sorrow awaits you…For you are so careful to clean the outside of the cup and the dish, but inside you are filthy—full of greed and self-indulgence! You frauds! You are like painted tombs or fancy coffins, which look beautiful on the outside but on the inside are full of the bones of the dead and everything unclean. Outwardly you look like righteous people, but inwardly your hearts are filled with hypocrisy and lawlessness. Matthew 23:25-29 NTL Paraphrased

IN A SINGLE DAY MY FALSE RELIGION AND MY WHOLE WORLD COLLAPSED

The Bible tells us that when our houses are built upon the solid rock of the Word of God and the storms of life come, our house will stand. The truth is that everything else except the Word of Jesus Christ is shifting, sinking sand. When the house of our life is built on sinking sand, it may stand for a while, but in the end it will collapse into ruin when trials come.

I had actually managed to survive with one foot on Jesus and one foot in my world of unrepentance and disobedience, continuing my sinfulness for quite a long time, but it doesn't last forever. After nine years into my life as a professing Christian and five years into my marriage, the unstable ground on which my success and happiness were reliant upon began to shift and shake. Trying to live your life with one foot on faith in Christ and one foot on continued wickedness simply does not work. Sooner or later your feet get so far apart that you cannot stop yourself from falling into ruin.

I had put my trust in my business savvy to provide for my family's future, but by 1981 my businesses were hemorrhaging thousands of dollars every month and we were accumulating a huge debt. It became obvious to me that we were going to lose everything and there was really nothing I could do to stop it from happening. I pulled farther and farther away from God and my wife, and I went further and further into old sinful ways as everything was collapsing around me.

The stress of the situation was further increased by the fact that my step-Dad had been diagnosed with an aggressive form of cancer and was languishing in hospital, dying a slow and painful death. Norm was far from perfect, but he had raised and taken care of me from the time I was five years old and I knew that he loved me as much as he was capable of. He was the only Dad I really knew. Now Mom and I were experiencing the strain and sorrow of helplessly watching him slowly waste away to less than ninety pounds as a result of the cancer.

Then one day in 1981 Dad's suffering was over. The hospital phoned and told us he was gone. Arrangements were made for his funeral to be held the following weekend, but I would never make it to my dad's funeral.

It was a Friday night, the night before my Dad's funeral when the ground of my own unrepentance and wickedness suddenly gave way from underneath me. Everything in my life suddenly collapsed. As a result of my sin, my five-year marriage was destroyed. My step-father was dead. My businesses were in ruins. I was deeply in debt with no income, and there was a real possibility of jail time lying ahead as a result of some of my evil behavior.

In a single night all of my feelings of shame and failure and sense of condemnation as a husband, father and provider for my family suddenly came to the surface like a critically open wound. I didn't know where to turn or what to do. It was more than I could handle spiritually or emotionally, so I ran. I got in my car and drove. I kept driving for hours, mile after mile, waffling back and forth between the only three options that I could think of.

The Devil was working overtime to try to pound it into my head that I was now at a three-way intersection, a three-way crossroad in my life. I could go back and try to start over, but that would almost certainly mean going to jail. I could keep running and try to start anew, or I could wait for a semi-trailer truck coming in the opposite direction and turn my car into its path. I am telling you the truth when I say that the strongest urge (by far) was the thought to kill myself and end it all. I was a terrible person. Nobody could love me, I thought, not even God, and the world would be better off without me.

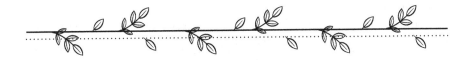

CHAPTER 7

Should We Believe God?

THE THREE WAY CROSS ROAD

I knew that my life had to change that very night but I did not know what to do or how to do it. So I continued driving for hundreds of miles as I reviewed the memories of my life and sorrowed over my sins. I was searching for an answer, searching for an escape from the person that I had become. I could turn the car around, go back to my wife and beg her to give me another chance to start over. I could just keep driving, run away from it all and begin a new life. Lastly, I was so ashamed of the things I had done and the way my life had turned out that I wanted to die. I thought that I deserved to die.

Really, the only thing that hindered me from taking my own life that night was not so much a fear of dying, but a fear of going to hell because of my sins. My parents did not know much about God but they knew enough to teach me that the wicked go to hell. My fear of that eternal consequence was just about the only thing that prevented me from giving in to the temptation to take my own life.

Nonetheless, this third voice, the voice of hopeless depression and loathing self-condemnation was the one that was fighting the hardest to impose itself upon my mind and my will. It was certainly the loudest. "You don't deserve to live. Commit suicide and end it all." For six hours I drove on and on, trying to decide what to do, fighting the urge to kill myself.

Yet, at the same time, I was praying and crying out to God for an answer as to why this was all happening to me.

I didn't realize it then, but I know now that Satan was still lying to me. He was still attempting to manipulate me by trying to convince me that these were the only three paths that I could take to get out of the situation. According to him there were only three directions that I could go. I did not understand at the time that Satan is a master of the three way cross road.

When Satan spoke with Adam and Eve in the Garden of Eden, he enticed them with three specific temptations to try to get them to embrace evil. He tempted them with pride (you shall be as gods). He tempted them with lustful desire (the forbidden fruit was pleasing to look at and good for food). He tempted them with greed.

God had given them a great abundance of food, all the food that they would ever need. All the food in the garden was theirs (with the exception of the fruit from that one tree). Yet, Adam and Eve fell from perfection and death entered human nature because they ignored God and listened to Satan. They believed what the Devil said, and it ruined their lives.

When Satan tempted Jesus in the wilderness at the beginning of Christ's ministry, the Devil enticed Jesus with three similar temptations. He encouraged Jesus to tempt God by throwing Himself off the roof of the temple, pointing out that the Word of God prophesied God would protect Jesus from harm (the pride of life). After 40 days of fasting, Jesus was hungry, so the Devil tempted Jesus with desire for food (the lust of the flesh). Then he took Jesus to a high place. He showed Jesus all the kingdoms of the world, promising to give them all to Him if Jesus would bow down and worship Satan (the lust of the eyes). Thankfully Jesus didn't obey Satan.

Now here I was in 1981 and Satan was doing exactly the same thing to me. He was doing his best to convince me that I only had three options. I could go back and try to start again. I could run away and try to start afresh or I could kill myself. Yet none of these answers seemed to be the right answer, the true answer, so I continued driving for no other reason than I did not know what else to do. As I drove I started pouring my heart out to God, begging for His help, praying for His guidance about what I should do next.

WE HAVE MORE THAN
THREE CHOICES!

I am telling you that there is more to Salvation than just believing in God and experiencing God's presence. There is a very important difference between **believing in God** and **trusting God, in believing what God has to say**.

In the beginning, the angels of God were created to dwell in the direct presence of God and yet a third of them still fell and will eventually end up in hell. In the beginning Adam and Eve obviously also believed in God and experienced God's presence because God walked and talked with them, but was that enough to keep them safe from evil? No it wasn't! Let's take a look at how Adam and Eve got into trouble in the Garden of Eden.

> But the LORD God warned him, "You may freely eat the fruit of every tree in the garden except the tree of the knowledge of good and evil. If you eat its fruit, you are sure to die... Gen. 2:16-17 NLT

> "You won't die!" the serpent replied to the woman. "God knows that your eyes will be opened as soon as you eat it, and you will be like God, knowing both good and evil." The woman was convinced. She saw that the tree was beautiful and its fruit looked delicious, and she wanted the wisdom it would give her. So she took some of the fruit and ate it. Then she gave some to her husband, who was with her, and he ate it, too. Gen. 3:4-6 NLT

Here we have the world's first example of two human beings just like you and me who believed in God. They believed that God existed and they experienced God's presence but that was not enough to keep them from dying. It was not enough to keep them out of hell. The real life and death questions in this scenario are "Yes, in the beginning, Adam and Eve believed in God, but did they trust God? Did they believe God's Word? Did they obey God?"

The above Scripture passage tells us the answer to these questions. They chose not to trust God. They chose not to believe God's Word. They chose not to obey God and the consequences of those choices are:

1. We all have evil within our nature
2. We all die
3. We are all already condemned to follow Satan into hell if we continue to serve him

Fortunately for Adam and Eve and all of the rest of us, God could not bear the thought of having all of His children separated from Him and condemned to hell for eternity. After they sinned, God came to Adam and Eve and had mercy and compassion toward them. God offered them a way of salvation if they wanted to repent and come back into God's family.

God explained to Adam and Eve that man must shed the innocent blood of animals and wear their skins as clothing as a reminder that mankind had brought evil and death into the world. God promised them that He would accept this ritual as a covering for humanity's sin until the time when mankind's Redeemer would be born of one of Eve's descendants. God also declared to Adam and Eve that the promised Redeemer would then crush Satan and his dominance over the human race. Right from the very beginning, mankind's path to salvation has always been through repentance, saved by God's grace through faith in His promise of a Redeemer

THE DIFFERENCE BETWEEN
ABEL AND CAIN

Adam and Eve were originally given a genuine opportunity to choose not to embrace evil. They had the free choice to trust God, believe God and obey Him. They could have chosen to reject evil and live forever. Did you know that the Word of God tells us that (contrary to what Satan wants you to believe) we all still have that same choice today?

Satan wants us to believe that because evil became part of our nature when Adam and Eve chose to embrace evil, mankind has lost our choice and ability to reject evil and turn back to our former inheritance of eternal life in God, but this is just another lie of the Devil.

Even though the knowledge of evil now resides within every human being, Satan cannot make us sin. He can only influence us toward evil through trials and temptations. He can only lie to try to convince us that we cannot stop sinning. He can only try to deceive us by telling us that we have no other paths to follow than to keep on sinning, but the Devil is a liar.

Even after Adam and Eve fell, God gave mankind an opportunity of salvation through repentance and faith in His promise of a Redeemer being born of one of Eve's descendants. The first two biological deaths on Earth were not human. They were animals, and The Bible does not specify which creatures were the first to die after evil entered man's domain but Genesis 3 does tell us that God Himself made Adam and Eve's first approved clothing out of animal skins.

Some suggest that it was God who killed the animals. It's possible, but I doubt that. Knowing Satan's evil heart, he probably caused some of the animals to drop dead as soon as Adam rejected God and Satan was released to introduce evil and death into man's dominion. However, the future shedding of innocent blood by man to make his own clothing would be required by God to cover the inner darkness that had now become part of man's being.

I believe that the Word of God indicates to us that Adam and Eve did listen to God and repent. I believe they turned away from evil and tried to teach their children to do the same because the Scriptures reveal that Abel did choose to believe God. However, Adam and Eve's firstborn son, Cain rejected God's Way of Salvation. In spite of God's expressed desire for Cain to repent and do the right thing, Cain continued to embrace and practice evil (see 1 John 3:12)

Cain wanted no part of God's bloody sacrifices to cover his sins. Instead, he tried to establish his own form of righteousness based on his own vain works. It was not really the content of Cain's offering that was the problem (as some suppose) but that Cain thought he could please God with gifts while he continued in his evil ways. Jesus said that Satan was a murderer and a liar right from the beginning and he is still lying to mankind today.

When Satan told Adam and Eve that they would not die if they ate from the tree of knowledge of good and evil, he was effectively trying to murder mankind. When they chose to believe the words of Satan rather than Father God, Satan succeeded in bringing death to the entire human race. By convincing Adam and Eve to believe and act on his lies, Satan was successful in murdering Adam and Eve and all of their descendants.

The Evolutionists are trying to convince you that death is an "evolved" process that has always been a part of human life, but that is also a lie. The Bible tells us that God holds Satan responsible for the mortal death of every human who has ever existed. It is presently Satan who has the power of death over humanity. However, God promises us that mankind can take a path in this life which conquers death and leads to eternal life, and Jesus our Savior shows us what this path is.

DO YOU BELIEVE IN GOD?

Listen to me dear reader! It took me nine years of pain and heartache to learn that believing in God and Jesus Christ is no guarantee of Salvation, but it does not have to be that way for you. There is a huge awakening going on right now in the Nation of Christianity. It is a renewal of faith that emphasizes believing in the gifts of the Holy Spirit and embracing the truths in God's Word.

I am all for this revival. I think that this renewal of faith in God's Word is a wonderful thing, but I am going to shock some of you by declaring to you that even if we believe in God and proclaim that Jesus is Lord and go to church and sense the presence of God and perform signs and wonders and miracles, it does not necessarily mean that we are on the road to Salvation.

The angels of God not only believe that God exists, they **know** that God exists because they were all created from the beginning to dwell in God's presence in the Third Heaven. Yet even though they all knew God existed and they all experienced God's direct presence, one third of them still embraced evil and were cast out of God's direct presence. They are all now on the path of eternal damnation, separation from God, and will all eventually end up in eternal Hell because they refused to depart from evil and their nature continued to deteriorate until, eventually, there was no good left in them.

God's Word says "Do you believe in God? The Devils also believe and tremble". There is more to Salvation than just believing in God and experiencing His presence. What about Adam and Eve? They believed in God. They experienced His presence. They walked and talked with God in the Garden of Eden, yet they were still responsible for bringing evil and death to the human race. What about Cain? He believed in God. He talked with God. God walked and talked with Cain and look how Cain ended up because he refused to depart from evil.

BELIEF IN GOD AND
EXPERIENCING GOD'S PRESENCE
IS ONLY THE STARTING POINT

Do you believe in God and Jesus Christ? It's a good start. It's the first step, but it is not Salvation. The Scriptures tell us that if anyone wants to come to God, they must first believe that God exists and is a rewarder of those who diligently seek Him, but there is more to true Christianity than just believing in God and Jesus Christ.

Right now, the nation of Christianity is undergoing what many people are referring to as the fifth spiritual Great Awakening. This spiritual awakening is based on a restoration of faith within the church to believe in the presence and ministry and gifts of the Holy Spirit. People are once again beginning to understand that the Holy Spirit and His gifts are still available to us as Christians today and should be pursued as a valuable blessing and aid to evangelism. This present Christian movement places great emphasis on pursuing and experiencing the presence of God and walking in obedience.

This is all good. We are headed in the right direction. The problem is that many have wrongly supposed that the manifestation of the gifts of the Holy Spirit and experiencing the presence of God is evidence of God's approval on our lives regardless of how ungodly our actual behavior is. The gifts of the Holy Spirit and the presence of God are treated like some sort of magic talisman. People think that the miracles of God are a mystical guarantee that everyone who shares these experiences will all be saved. I am telling you that it's simply not true. There's more to it than this.

Hear me, dear readers! Many professing Christians today are making exactly the same mistakes in their lives that Israel once made and I once made. The gifts of the Holy Spirit and the presence of God are all good, but they are no guarantee of Salvation. They are not a spiritual seal of God's approval.

Israel experienced the miracles of God for forty years in the wilderness and many still perished. The disciple Judas was directly involved in healing people and casting demons out of people for a while, but he was not saved. Judas and many of Christ's other peers all lived and experienced miracles and the direct presence of God in their lives in the person of Jesus Christ, yet it did not save them. Likewise, the Bible tells us that many professing Christians will one day stand before God in the future having done miracles only to hear God say "I do not know you. Depart from Me you evildoers."

The first step toward salvation is indeed to believe that God exists and that He is a rewarder of those who diligently seek Him. The second step is to seek God out, to desire to dwell in His presence, to desire to talk to God and have God manifest Himself to us through the Holy Spirit and His gifts, but that still does not bring us to the place of Salvation. The Word of God clearly **tells us** what will bring us to the path of salvation:

> "Not everyone who says to me, 'Lord, Lord,' will enter the kingdom of heaven, but only the one who does the will of my Father who is in heaven. Many will say to me on that day, 'Lord, Lord, did we not prophesy in your name and in your name drive out demons and in your name perform many miracles?' Then I will tell them plainly, 'I never knew you. Away from me, you evildoers!' Matthew 7:21-23 NIV

YOU BELIEVE IN GOD, BUT DO YOU ACTUALLY BELIEVE WHAT GOD SAYS?

What does it really mean to you when you say that you believe in God and Jesus Christ? Do you believe God's Word when He tells us that not everyone who proclaims "Jesus is Lord" will enter the kingdom of heaven? Do you believe Jesus when He tells us that only those who do the will of His Father will enter the kingdom of heaven? Do you trust and believe Jesus when He tells us that He will reject evildoers, even if they have ministered and performed miracles in His name?

Take the example of Cain and Abel. Both believed in God, both talked with God, but one man **listened to** God, **trusted God**, **believed God**, **obeyed God**, and the other did not. God certainly gave Cain the opportunity to change. Didn't God talk to Cain personally and give Cain the opportunity to repent and do the right thing?

> "Why are you so angry?" the LORD asked Cain. "Why do you look so dejected? You will be accepted if you do what is right. But if you refuse to do what is right, then watch out! Sin is crouching at the door, eager to control you. But you must subdue it and be its master." Gen 4:6-7 NLT

Cain was lost to Satan because he refused to repent and do the right things. Cain believed in God, but he refused to trust and obey God. Then, if we move ahead to Enoch and Noah's generation, we see that the presence of God was still available to mankind if they wanted it. God was still personally walking and talking with people in the days of Enoch and Noah:

> After the birth of Methuselah, Enoch lived in close fellowship with God...walking in close fellowship with God. Then one day he disappeared, because God took him. Gen 5:22-24 NLT

> This is the account of Noah and his family. Noah was a righteous man, the only blameless person living on earth at the time, and he walked in close fellowship with God... so God said to Noah...

Genesis 6:9-13 NLT

The opportunity was still available for human beings to walk and talk with God for almost a thousand years after God created Adam and Eve, but by then the entire world was going Cain's way. They believed in God. They believed that God existed, but they wanted to worship God **their** way. They were all busy establishing their own concepts of righteousness. Yet it was not righteousness at all.

God's Word tells us that their thoughts became evil continually. They did not believe God and they did not obey God anymore. Neither would they believe the words of the prophets that God sent to warn them, and so they all perished in the flood. God's way of Salvation was not complicated. All they had to do to be saved was listen to Enoch, Methuselah and Noah, repent and get aboard the Ark with Noah and they would have survived. Yet, even though they believed **in** God, they refused to **believe God** and they refused to **obey what God said** and so they perished.

CHAPTER 8

Trust and Obey God

ABRAHAM BELIEVED
AND OBEYED GOD

Let's go ahead now a couple of thousand years to a man called Abraham and we see that God is still talking personally to those who are willing to listen. The Book of Romans tells us that what saved Abraham was not that he believed **in** God, but that he **believed what God said** and lived his life accordingly.

> For what does the Scripture say? Abraham believed God, and it was accounted to him for righteousness. Romans 4:3 NKJV

If we go ahead two more generations to Jacob, who is also called Israel, the father and founder of the nation of Israel, we see that God is still talking to mankind. This time God speaks to former sinner Jacob in a dream in Genesis 28, and Jacob **believes** God and vows to serve Him. Then we go ahead to when Jacob is 110 years old and close to dying. He calls his son Joseph and gives him this blessing for his grandsons:

> Then he blessed Joseph and said, "**May the God before whom my grandfather Abraham and my father,**

Isaac, walked— the God who has been my shepherd all my life, to this very day, the Angel who has redeemed me from all harm— may he bless these boys. May they preserve my name and the names of Abraham and Isaac, and may their descendants multiply greatly throughout the earth." Genesis 48:15-16 NLT

So once again we see that Abraham and Isaac walked with God and Jacob trusted God as his shepherd to guide him throughout his life. They all believed what God said, and obeyed God, and it was counted to them for righteousness.

MOSES TRUSTED AND OBEYED GOD

Next we move ahead in history a couple of more generations to a man named Moses and we find out that God still spoke directly to people in Moses' day. God spoke to Moses from within the burning bush and Moses chose to believe God and obey Him. In the end, Moses delivers the entire nation of Israel from the tyranny of Egypt. Trusting and believing God for miracle after miracle, Moses led Israel all the way to the Jordan River, to the very borders of the land that God had promised to the descendants of Abraham.

Furthermore, Moses accomplished all this in spite of the fact that God's people repeatedly insisted on returning back to their own understanding, their own concepts of righteousness and their old wicked and sinful ways.

Finally, when Israel refused to believe God's promise that He will help them defeat the heathen to claim their inheritance, God decreed that the whole nation would have to wander in the wilderness until that entire generation of adults was dead except for Joshua and Caleb. They were the only two in the whole nation who had believed what God had said and were willing to act on it, and they would be the only ones permitted to enter the Promised Land from that generation of God's own chosen people:

"But even after all he did, you refused to trust the LORD your God, who goes before you looking for the best places to camp, guiding you with a pillar of fire by night and a pillar of cloud by day. "When the LORD heard your complaining, he became very angry. So he solemnly swore, 'Not one of you from this wicked generation will live to see the good land I swore to give your ancestors,

Deuteronomy 1:32-35 NLT

THE NATION OF ISRAEL WAS CONQUERED BECAUSE THEY DID NOT TRUST AND OBEY GOD

It took 40 years of God's miraculous provision in the desert wilderness for that bunch to die off and the next generation of Israel to learn to trust God enough to go and take the land that God had promised them. Even then, many soon forgot about God again. The ranks of the disobedient and unbelieving in Israel rapidly regrew in the Promised Land until God finally withdrew His protection from Israel and the whole nation was taken into slavery by Assyria.

Why? It happened because even though they knew God, they refused to repent and obey Him. They continued to sin against God and their fellow man. They stubbornly refused to turn away from evil.

This disaster came upon the people of Israel **because they ... sinned against the LORD their God,** who had brought them safely out of Egypt and had rescued them from the power of Pharaoh, the king of Egypt. They had followed the practices of the pagan nations the LORD had driven from the land ahead of them, as well as the practices the kings of Israel had introduced. **The people of Israel had also secretly done many things that were not pleasing to the LORD their God**... But the Israelites would not listen. They were as stubborn as their ancestors who had refused to believe in the LORD their God. They rejected his decrees and the covenant he had made with their ancestors, and they despised all his warnings...

So **while these new residents worshiped the LORD, they also worshiped their idols. And to this day their descendants do the same.** 2 Kings 17: 7-41 NLT

Now go and write down these words. Write them in a book. They will stand until the end of time as a witness that **these people are stubborn rebels who refuse to pay attention to the LORD's instructions.** They tell the seers, "Stop seeing visions!" They tell the prophets, "Don't tell us what is right. Tell us nice things. Tell us lies. Forget all this gloom. Get off your narrow path. Stop telling us about your 'Holy One of Israel.'" This is the reply of the Holy One of Israel: "**Because you despise what I tell you and trust instead in oppression and lies, calamity will come upon you suddenly**— like a bulging wall that bursts and falls. In an instant it will collapse and come crashing down. You will be smashed like a piece of pottery— shattered so completely that there won't be a piece big enough to carry coals from a fireplace or a little water from the well." This is what the Sovereign LORD, the Holy One of Israel, says: "**Only in returning to me and resting in me will you be saved**. Isaiah 30:8-15 NLT

Brothers and sisters, my heart's desire and prayer to God for the Israelites is that they may be saved.

For I can testify about them that they are zealous for God, but their zeal is not based on knowledge. **Since they did not know the righteousness of God and sought to establish their own, they did not submit to God's righteousness.**

Romans 10:1-3 NIV

You have just read God's explanation as to why Israel was still a conquered and occupied nation when Jesus came on the scene. This is why, when John the Baptist and Jesus and the Apostles began their ministries in Israel, they all focused on the same basic message "Repent (turn away from your wickedness) and start trusting and believing God's promises.

This was God's main message to Israel. Furthermore, it is the same message that Jesus and the Apostles preach to those seeking Salvation today. Repent! Believe what God has to say about Jesus Christ being mankind's Redeemer and follow Him. Walk as He walked. God's message to Israel and to every person reading this book is to turn away from evil. We must realize that **if we are not capable of turning away from evil, then God would not be commanding us to do it**.

Once we begin to understand this very basic principle of what God wants us to do to come to Salvation, it then becomes a matter of who we are going to choose to believe. Are we going to continue to believe the liar Satan who has been ruining our lives up to this point? Are we going to keep on sinning? Or are we going to turn away from evil in trust in God, The Holy Spirit and Jesus Christ as our Savior to help us overcome our sinful nature through the presence and power of the Holy Spirit?

CHAPTER 9

God's Grace is No License to Sin

THE DISPENSATION OF GRACE WILL
NOT SAVE US IF WE KEEP SINNING

You may have heard professing Christians declare that since Jesus died for our sins we are now no longer under the Law but under grace. This is certainly a true statement if you understand what it means. What it means is that, even though we are all worthy of death because none have kept the law, we accept that Jesus Christ has paid the price in full for the sins of all who desire to return to God and accept Jesus as our Savior.

Today we do not condemn people to death for idolatry, blasphemy, stealing, lying, fornication, or any other sexual sin as was the case under the Law during Old Testament times. In Canada, we no longer put people to death even for murder, but that does not mean that Christians can continue to participate in this kind of evil behavior. It does not mean that there will not be consequences for professing Christians who are rejecting God's Word and continuing to embrace evil.

Dear friends, if we deliberately continue sinning after we have received knowledge of the truth, there is no longer any sacrifice that will cover these sins. There is only the terrible expectation of God's judgment and the raging fire that will consume his enemies. For anyone who refused to obey the Law of Moses was put to death without mercy on the testimony of two or three witnesses. Just think how much worse the punishment will be for those who have trampled on the Son of God, and have treated the blood of the covenant, which made us holy, as if it were common and unholy, and have insulted and disdained the Holy Spirit who brings God's mercy to us.

Hebrews 10:26-29 NLT

There were a lot of people in Israel who opposed Jesus and His teachings because they supposed that their self-righteousness and religious rituals balanced God's scales enough to make up for continued evil behavior in their lives, but Jesus refused to accept their false piety and unrepentance.

About this time Jesus was informed that Pilate had murdered some people from Galilee as they were offering sacrifices at the Temple. "Do you think those Galileans were worse sinners than all the other people from Galilee?" Jesus asked. "Is that why they suffered? Not at all! And you will perish, too, unless you repent of your sins and turn to God. And what about the eighteen people who died when the tower in Siloam fell on them? Were they the worst sinners in Jerusalem? No, and I tell you again **that unless you repent, you will perish, too.**" Luke 13:1-5 NLT

Then Jesus went through the towns and villages, teaching as he made his way to Jerusalem. Someone asked him, "Lord, are only a few people going to be saved?" He said to them, "**Make every effort to enter through the narrow door**, because many, I tell you, will try to enter and will not be able to. Once the owner of the house gets up and closes the door, you will stand outside knocking and pleading, 'Sir, open the door for us.' "But he will answer, 'I don't know you or where you come from.' "Then you will say, 'We ate and drank with you, and you taught in our streets.' "But he will reply, '**I don't know**

**you or where you come from. Away from me, all you
evildoers!'** "There will be weeping there, and gnashing
of teeth, when you see Abraham, Isaac and Jacob and all
the prophets in the kingdom of God, **but you yourselves
thrown out**. Luke 13:22-28 NLT

GOD FORGIVES OUR SIN
BUT HE ALSO COMMANDS
US TO STOP SINNING!

Jesus taught that there would be many who would try to enter the
narrow door to Salvation but would not be able to get through the door. He
was explaining to us that no one can get through the door of Salvation via
performing good works or religious practices if we reject God's command
for us to repent and turn away from doing evil.

When God's Word tells us that Jesus is the door and Jesus is the way
to Salvation, it is talking about more than just realizing and proclaiming
that Jesus is God's promised Redeemer of the human race. If we want to
be saved, God expects us to repent and follow the example and instructions
for Salvation that Jesus Christ has provided for us.

> Then he said to the crowd, "If any of you wants to be
> my follower, you must turn from your selfish ways, take
> up your cross daily, and follow me.
> Luke 9:23 NLT

> My dear children, I am writing this to you so that you
> will not sin. But if anyone does sin, we have an advocate
> who pleads our case before the Father. He is Jesus Christ,
> the one who is truly righteous. He himself is the sacrifice
> that atones for our sins—and not only our sins but the
> sins of all the world. And we can be sure that we know
> him if we obey his commandments. If someone claims,
> "I know God," but doesn't obey God's commandments,
> that person is a liar and is not living in the truth. But

those who obey God's word truly show how completely they love him. That is how we know we are living in him. Those who say they live in God should live their lives as Jesus did… And now, dear children, remain in fellowship with Christ so that when he returns, you will be full of courage and not shrink back from him in shame. Since we know that Christ is righteous, we also know that all who do what is right are God's children. 1 John 2:1-29 NLT

"So why do you keep calling me 'Lord, Lord!' when you don't do what I say? I will show you what it's like when someone comes to me, listens to my teaching, and then follows it. It is like a person building a house who digs deep and lays the foundation on solid rock. When the floodwaters rise and break against that house, it stands firm because it is well built. But anyone who hears and doesn't obey is like a person who builds a house without a foundation. When the floods sweep down against that house, it will collapse into a heap of ruins." Luke 6:46-49 NLT

JESUS STILL DOES NOT WANT US TO
JUDGE AND CONDEMN OTHERS

Most people have heard about the occasion when the religious leaders of Israel caught a woman in the act of adultery and took her into custody. The Law of the land at the time stated that adulterers were to be put to death by stoning, so they brought this woman by force before Jesus. They threw her at His feet, looking for blood.

These corrupt religious leaders were hoping that Jesus would condemn her to death. They could use the situation to turn the people against Jesus, but the Word of God tells us that Jesus was not sent to condemn the world but to show us the path to eternal life. The first thing that Jesus did on that day was to deal with the hypocrisy of those who were more than willing to stone this woman to death even though they all knew that they had sin in their own lives

As he was speaking, the teachers of religious law and the Pharisees brought a woman who had been caught in the act of adultery. They put her in front of the crowd. "Teacher," they said to Jesus, "this woman was caught in the act of adultery. The Law of Moses says to stone her. What do you say?" They were trying to trap him into saying something they could use against him, but Jesus stooped down and wrote in the dust with his finger. They kept demanding an answer, so he stood up again and said, "All right, but let the one who has never sinned throw the first stone!" Then he stooped down again and wrote in the dust. When the accusers heard this, they slipped away one by one, beginning with the oldest, until only Jesus was left in the middle of the crowd with the woman. John 8:3-9 NLT

JESUS DOES NOT CONDEMN US.
WE ARE CONDEMNED ALREADY

There is much more to be learned from the story of the adulterous woman than just the fact that Jesus embarrassed her accusers and spared her from being condemned to death. Many unlearned people have the wrong idea about Christianity and Jesus Christ. They think that God sends people to hell just because they reject Jesus. That is a terrible distortion of the truth that God wants us to understand about heaven and hell.

Rejecting Jesus doesn't send people to hell. God's Word tells us that the entire human race is condemned to be eternally separated from God already because we are all sinners. We have all chosen to embrace evil to certain degrees in our lives. God's purpose in sending us Jesus Christ was to send us someone who has the power and authority and desire to save and redeem us from that state of condemnation that the whole world **already exists in**.

The truth is that we all have sin on our life's record. Every single one of the adulterous woman's accusers were under the same condemnation that she was. In God's eyes, they were all worthy of death. They did not even have the integrity to bring the man she had sinned with before Jesus so that he could also be "judged". Once they realized that their hypocrisy was exposed, her accusers' consciences shamed them. Gradually they all retreated away from the Son of God and back to the darkness from which they had come.

> For God so loved the world that he gave his one and only Son, that whoever believes in him shall not perish but have eternal life. For God did not send his Son into the world to condemn the world, but to save the world through him. Whoever believes in him is not condemned, but whoever does not believe stands condemned already because they have not believed in the name of God's one and only Son. This is the verdict: Light has come into the world, but people loved darkness instead of light because their deeds were evil. Everyone who does evil hates the light, and will not come into the light for fear that their deeds will be exposed. But whoever lives by the truth comes into the light... John 3:16-21 NIV

CHAPTER 10

Already Condemned

WE ARE ALL LIKE THE
ADULTEROUS WOMAN

When it comes to guilt, God's Word declares that we are all guilty and worthy of death. Yet we can all learn a lot from the story of this adulterous woman. First, her own sin had resulted in her being taken into captivity. She was no longer free. Second, her sin had placed her under the sentence of death and there was no escape for her. If Jesus had not been present to intercede for her, this woman would certainly have been put to death.

Another important thing to note here is that the woman did not even willingly come to Jesus on her own. I am sure that she was terrified as her accusers took her by force and then tossed her at the feet of Jesus like she was a piece of human garbage to be disposed of. However, the leaders had not counted on the fact that Jesus loved her. The truth is that Jesus was willing to set her free and then die for this woman's salvation and our salvation even while we were all yet sinners.

> When we were utterly helpless, Christ came at just the right time and died for us sinners. Now, most people would not be willing to die for an upright person, though someone might perhaps be willing to die for a person who is especially good. But God showed his great love

for us by sending Christ to die for us while we were still sinners. And since we have been made right in God's sight by the blood of Christ, he will certainly save us from God's condemnation. For since our friendship with God was restored by the death of his Son while we were still his enemies, we will certainly be saved through the life of his Son. So now we can rejoice in our wonderful new relationship with God because our Lord Jesus Christ has made us friends of God.

Romans 5:6-11 NLT

One of the main lessons to be learned from the story of Christ's encounter with the adulterous woman is that even when we are not thinking of God or looking for God, Jesus still loves us. He still forgives us. He does not want to judge us. At the time that Christ met her, this woman was not looking for Jesus or for spiritual salvation. She was brought forcibly before Jesus and dumped at His feet by her accusers.

There was no question that the adulterous woman was guilty of walking in sin, yet Jesus did not condemn her. He showed her mercy and forgiveness. He set her free from death, but Jesus did not stop there. He then gave her a very specific command to **go and sin no more,** and knowledge of His love for her gave her the spiritual strength to go and do just that.

CHRIST'S LOVE SETS US FREE, FREE TO STOP SINNING

This is actually the main point of the message that Jesus is trying to convey to us in the story. I was once like many professing Christians today who continue to stumble around in habitual sinful behavior, not understanding that they can be set free from the chains of sin that have held us captive for all of our lives. Through the story of the adulterous woman Jesus is showing this woman and all of us an open door and commanding us to go through it.

Jesus is not giving mankind advice in this passage. He is not showing us an optional avenue of behavior that we can choose to follow or choose to ignore. Jesus sets us free from our condemnation and death sentence but then He **commands** us to **go and sin no more** and Jesus would not require us to do this without empowering us through the Holy Spirit to be able to obey His instructions.

> So now there is no condemnation for those who belong to Christ Jesus. And because you belong to him, the power of the life-giving Spirit has freed you from the power of sin that leads to death... God did what the law could not do. He sent his own Son in a body like the bodies we sinners have. And in that body God declared an end to sin's control over us by giving his Son as a sacrifice for our sins. He did this so that the just requirement of the law would be fully satisfied for us, who no longer follow our sinful nature but instead follow the Spirit. Those who are dominated by the sinful nature think about sinful things, but those who are controlled by the Holy Spirit think about things that please the Spirit. So letting your sinful nature control your mind leads to death. But letting the Spirit control your mind leads to life and peace...Therefore, dear brothers and sisters, you have no obligation to do what your sinful nature urges you to do. For if you live by its dictates, you will die. But if through the power of the Spirit you put to death the deeds of your sinful nature, you will live. For all who are led by the Spirit of God are children of God. Romans 8:1-14 NLT

Are you hearing what the Spirit of God is saying to us here? If we claim to be Christians, we need to believe God's promise that the power of Christ's life giving Spirit frees us from the power of sin that leads to death. Through Christ, God declares that sin no longer has control over those who refuse to follow our sinful nature but allow ourselves to be controlled by the Holy Spirit. Thus we no longer have any obligation to do what our sinful natures urge us to do. We can be free!

THERE IS NO CONDEMNATION
FOR FOLLOWERS OF CHRIST

This is a perfectly accurate statement if we truly understand what it means. Unfortunately, it is a Scripture that is often twisted and wrongly used by many who claim to be Christians yet are continuing to allow our old sinful nature to control our minds, our speech and our behavior.

I implore you to listen to the truth about this. We are not going to get away with taking one part of the Word of God out of context and ignoring the part that says that if we continue to live by the dictates of our sinful nature we will die. Let's use the adulterous woman as an example. Jesus loved her. He did not condemn her. He showed mercy and compassion toward her. He forgave her and delivered her from her death sentence and set her free. Then He told her to **go and sin no more**.

Now think carefully about this. What do you think would have happened if this woman had then chosen to ignore the instruction of Jesus to go and sin no more? If the woman refused to obey Jesus and returned to her old sinful ways, she would have put herself back under the condemnation of the Law and the next time that she was caught in the act, she would have been put to death as a transgressor. When we are repentant, Christ sets us free from the law of sin and death, but when we are unrepentant we put ourselves back under the law of sin and death. The Word of God tells us that the Law is not for the righteous. The Law and those who administer the Law are supposed to exist to be a terror to those who are determined to do evil. Christians need to get this.

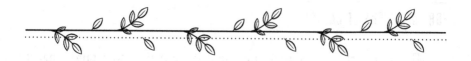

CHAPTER 11

God Still Speaks

REPENTANCE OPENS THE DOOR

Yes, Jesus is the only door to eternal life, but God's message to mankind from Genesis to Revelation has never changed. It has always been "repent and believe God's promise of a Redeemer". Yes, Jesus is the only door to our Salvation, but repentance (turning away from evil) is what moves us from darkness to light in order to be able to see the door. Repentance is what brings us to the door and repentance is what God requires of us if we want to enter through the door that leads to salvation. We cannot sneak into the Kingdom of God without repentance, thinking that it is something that we can do later.

Every book and every prophet in the Old Testament from Abel to John the Baptist reminds humanity that we need to repent and believe in God's promise of the coming Redeemer. Then Jesus came along preaching "Repent. **I am the Redeemer**. I am the Messiah". Then the Apostles came along preaching "Repent, Jesus is not only the Redeemer and Messiah of Israel, He is the Savior of the entire world".

It is astounding to me that there are so many professing Christians who have no trouble hearing the last part of God's message which says that Jesus is our Savior, yet are totally deaf to the first part of God's message commanding us to repent and turn away from evil. Yes, Jesus is the only door to our salvation, but **repentance is the only way to open the door and pass through.** After that, Jesus will show us the way to walk.

Following Jesus in repentant obedience is the only way we can stay on the narrow path that ends in Salvation and eternal life as children of God in God's Kingdom.

I HAD TO LEARN THAT GOD'S WORD
APPLIES TO ME PERSONALLY

Even though I had called myself a Christian before that day in 1981, I had been trying to live my life by vain confidence in myself according to my own warped concepts of righteousness. It was not until I hit rock bottom in my life that I understood that this kind of Christianity simply does not work. It is not true Christianity. It is a false gospel, a false way that does not lead to Salvation.

Have you ever heard someone say that they tried Christianity and it didn't work for them? That's because they tried a false Christianity. They tried one that doesn't include true repentance, turning away from evil and totally putting your faith and trust in God. Until we set our sights on loving God with all our heart and all our soul and all our mind, we are **still following Satan**. Until we choose to follow Jesus in obedience to His commands, we are still living our lives in servitude to Satan and are under the laws of sin and death.

I now realize that God had allowed me to get to that low place in my life in 1981 in order to be truly set free. I finally reached the place where I had to admit that it was not God's fault that my life was in a shambles. It was my own fault because I had not fully trusted God. I had not believed God. I had not been fully obedient to God.

My problem was that I had tried to serve God and yet still keep some of my sin. I thought that I was independent and free at the time, but at last I came to the place when I realized that I wasn't free. I was still a prisoner to sin and Satan. It simply does not work to try to have one foot in the Kingdom of God and one foot in unrepentance and ungodliness.

So the LORD must wait for you to come to him so he can show you his love and compassion. For the LORD is a faithful God. Blessed are those who wait for his help. O people of Zion, who live in Jerusalem, you will weep no more. He will be gracious if you ask for help. He will surely respond to the sound of your cries. Isaiah 30:18-19 NLT

I prayed to the LORD, and he answered me. He freed me from all my fears...In my desperation I prayed, and the LORD listened; he saved me from all my troubles... Come, my children, and listen to me...Does anyone want to live a life that is long and prosperous? Then keep your tongue from speaking evil and your lips from telling lies! Turn away from evil and do good. Search for peace, and work to maintain it. The eyes of the LORD watch over those who do right; his ears are open to their cries for help. But the LORD turns his face against those who do evil; he will erase their memory from the earth. The LORD hears his people when they call to him for help. He rescues them from all their troubles. The LORD is close to the broken hearted; he rescues those whose spirits are crushed. Calamity will surely destroy the wicked, and those who hate the righteous will be punished. But the LORD will redeem those who serve him. No one who takes refuge in him will be condemned. Psalm 34:4-22 NLT

THE PATH OF REPENTANCE AND
OBEDIENCE HAS ALWAYS EXISTED

Ever since God spoke to Adam and Eve in the Garden of Eden, the door of repentance and the path of choosing to return to a life of trusting and obeying God has always been available to mankind but I never understood this for the first 28 years of my life. Blinded by Satan's deception, I did not comprehend or believe that I could stop sinning and I did not really grasp that God **requires me** to stop sinning.

On that day in 1981 I finally understood that this was the answer that I had been looking for. It was the piece of the puzzle that had always been missing from my religion and my life. The Bible explains in simple language where Adam and Eve went wrong and why my own life was lying in ruins at that moment in time.

I had made the same mistake that Adam and Eve made. I had not trusted in the Lord with all my heart. I had not shunned all evil. I had not fully submitted to God. I tried to build my life through leaning on my own wisdom and my own perceptions of good works and righteousness and in the end everything that I had built had collapsed into rubble.

God had spoken to me Spirit to spirit in 1972 declaring that He had spared my life. In 1972 I came to the revelation that God existed. Then later on I learned that Jesus was the Savior of the World and I wanted Him to be my Savior. Without proper Christian teaching and guidance, I mistakenly thought that this meant that everything was OK between myself and God. Yet, because I was unrepentant, I was still a slave to Satan without even realizing it.

The Devil convinced me that I was incapable of being set free of all of my sins and addictions. I listened to his lies telling me that continued wickedness in parts of my life would not destroy me. "You will not die!" the Devil promised. However, my sin did destroy my life and listening to Satan almost drove me to suicide. It was not until God allowed me to come to that crossroad in 1981 that I truly understood what Matthew is talking about when it says:

> Because strait is the gate, and narrow is the way, which leadeth unto life, and few there be that find it. Matthew 7:14 KJV

This is not some new teaching. Right after Adam and Eve made their original choice, God had mercy on them. Mankind would still have to experience mortal death because of the evil that now resides in our nature but God also gave man an offer of redemption from the hell that would consist of eternal subservience to Satan.

God encouraged Adam and Eve to repent (turn away from evil and back to God) promising that one of Eve's descendants would become the Redeemer for the entire human race. Through the Redeemer, God promised that all who put their faith in Him would be adopted back into God's family. To make it happen, all man had to do was repent and obey God.

GOD FORGIVES ALL OUR SINS, BUT EXPECTS US TO REPENT.

I have learned that it is very important for us to listen carefully to the Word of God and obey Him. How we respond to God today can affect our lives for many years to come.

The marital relationship between myself and my first wife started out in an ungodly way, a sinful way, but God is a forgiving God. We started off badly, but there is no doubt in my mind that if I had learned God's way of Salvation back then, if I had repented of my wicked ways and taught my family to do the same and follow Jesus Christ, God would have forgiven us and redeemed us as a family even though we started off on the wrong road.

I believe that this is true for every person reading this book as well. Is your previous life a mess because of bad behavior? Turn away from evil now. It's not too late. God will still forgive you and help you start over. How do I know that? I know this is true because there is not any sin in existence that God is not willing to forgive if we turn away from evil and back to God again. God forgave Adam and Eve for bringing evil and death into the world in the first place. Even after such a terrible transgression, God still offered them a path to salvation as a couple.

What about King David? The Bible tells us of King David spying on Bathsheba while she was bathing naked. David became so inflamed by his adulterous lust for her that he sent her husband into battle and ordered his soldiers to abandon him to the enemy so that he would be slain. David committed murder so that he could commit adultery. Yet God still forgave David when he later on sincerely repented and turned back to the Lord again.

> I have found David the son of Jesse, a man after mine own heart, which shall fulfil all my will.
> Acts 13:22 KJV

That does not mean that there would not be long-lasting consequences during and after David's lifetime for his past sins. There would be, but God still forgave David. If you want to know what it was about Jesse's son David that caused God to honor him as a man after God's own heart in spite of some of David's early failures, you'll find the answer in the Psalms of David. Here we find that even though David sinned grievously early in life, David eventually learned to trust God:

Psalm 31:14 NIV - But I trust in You Lord

Psalm 34:22 NKJV - None of those who trust in Him shall be condemned.

Psalm 118:8 NKJV - It is better to trust in the Lord than to put confidence in man.

I was misled by my own vanity and my own sinful heart as a young man. Even though I had acknowledged God's existence and accepted Jesus as the Savior of humanity, I had not learned to trust, believe and obey what God says to us.

Whenever a conflict arose between the Word of God and what I wanted to think, say or do, I had been placing my confidence in my own abilities and wisdom. I chose to continue to follow a sinful path convinced this would bring me love, joy, peace, success and fulfilment in my life. In the end it was my twisted confidence in myself (rather than in God) that destroyed both me and my family.

NINE YEARS OF SEARCHING FOR
GOD IN ALL THE WRONG PLACES

During the 1970's I had become aware of God's presence and was endeavoring to learn about the Lord. The problem was, I had not grasped that knowing about God and knowing what God has to say is not the same as determining to develop a personal relationship with God through repentance, trust, faith and obedience.

Spiritual blindness is a strange thing. In those days I simply could not see the truth and I had no one to teach me as I am now teaching others. I understand now that it is possible to have tons of Scripture memorized, and go to church to sing and pray and practice all kinds of religious rituals and traditions, and claim to be Christian, but still end up far from God.

If we refuse to walk in obedience and apply God's Word to our personal lives, we are only deceiving ourselves. The Bible actually tells us that those who try to justify continuing wickedness in our own lives by comparing our lives to the lives of other people are not really praying to God when we pray. We are actually praying to ourselves. We are trying to justify our own sins by praying to a God of our own making.

> Two men went to the Temple to pray. One was a Pharisee, and the other was a despised tax collector. The Pharisee stood by himself and prayed this prayer: 'I thank you, God, that I am not a sinner like everyone else. For I don't cheat, I don't sin, and I don't commit adultery. I'm certainly not like that tax collector! I fast twice a week, and I give you a tenth of my income.' "But the tax collector stood at a distance and dared not even lift his eyes to heaven as he prayed. Instead, he beat his chest in sorrow, saying, 'O God, be merciful to me, for I am a sinner.' I tell you, this sinner, not the Pharisee, returned home justified before God... Luke 18:10-14 NLT

MY SINFUL LIFE THREW ME
AT THE FEET OF JESUS

When I was driving along the highway that fateful day in 1981 all of my blindness and false pride was stripped away from me. I realized that I was a sinner deserving of death. In fact Satan was doing his best to pressure me to take my own life, but I did not really want to die. I wanted to live! I did not want to continue serving Satan in hell for the rest of eternity. I wanted to be with God. I wanted to overcome evil in my life. I wanted to live for God and be obedient to God, but I just did not know how to do it. In fact I knew I couldn't do it on my own.

The weight of my sin and guilt was so heavy upon me that I felt that I was being crushed emotionally and spiritually to the point of death. I could hardly breathe. With all that was in me I started crying out to God to be merciful to me, to lift this burden from my heart and help me to change.

Then something happened. All of a sudden I became so overwhelmed by such a sense of God's presence and His love for me that I began to weep uncontrollably in repentance. This was not normal crying. It was agonizing, soul-wrenching roars and groans that came from the deepest recesses of my being. It was so intense that it felt like my chest was being crushed and I could barely see to drive anymore. I pulled into the small town of Williams Lake looking for someplace to park until I could regain my composure and function normally again.

It was early Saturday morning by then and the town was all but deserted so I just picked a random parking stall on the main street. I pulled into it, and bowed my head on the steering wheel for a long time, continuing to cry and pray until at last I regained my composure. I am not sure how long I remained bowed over the steering wheel experiencing wave after wave of God's love, mercy and forgiveness, but it was a long time. Eventually things started to fade until the Holy Spirit began ministering to me. For the second time in my life I had the assurance that God was speaking to me, and this is what I heard:

HEARING THE VOICE OF GOD

"You are at a crossroad in your life, but it is not the three-way crossroad that the Devil has presented to you. **There is a fourth path and it is the only path that leads to eternal life.** The reason that you are in your present situation is that you have never truly repented. You have never fully turned away from evil and chosen to trust and follow Me. Now the Devil wants to totally destroy you. If you commit suicide tonight, you will die lost and be forever subjugated to the father that you have been serving.

Neither will it profit you to go back and start over, or keep running away. At this crossroads in your life, all paths that do not lead directly to Me are actually leading you further away from Me. If you keep following them, in the end they will all eventually lead to destruction and the same lost destination.

The choices that you have been considering seem to be three different paths, but wide is the road and broad is the way that leads to destruction, and straight is the gate and narrow is the path that leads to eternal life. In the end, all paths except one lead to the same destination, eternal servitude to the evil father that you have chosen to believe and follow.

Without repentance, the desire, greed and pride of humanity will always bring mankind to the same destination of eternal separation from God and they will forge many chains of bondage and torment along the way. Yet do not despair. I have not abandoned you. There has always been a fourth path for man to take, the path that Jesus took. It is the only one that will truly change your life and set you free. You need to truly repent and follow Jesus."

Finally I understood what God is saying to me, to the entire human race. There is no other way for us to be saved aside from fully turning away from evil. We must respond in faith to God's promise of a Redeemer and choose to fully follow Christ in obedience.

It's not that we will never stumble during our journey back to God. We will still sometimes make mistakes in the things that we think and say and do. We will all fail at times. God knows that. God knows that none of us are perfect, but God requires that we have a truly repentant heart and endeavor to do the best we can to listen to the daily guidance of the Holy Spirit who is the one who enables us to follow and obey Jesus Christ in our journey back to Father God.

The truth is that we are all only spiritual children learning to walk with Jesus. When we do stumble along the way, Jesus still loves us. His hand will always be there to lift us up and help us stand again, but habitual sinners will not get away with pulling their hands away from Jesus and continuing to walk in wickedness forever. Eventually, those who love the darkness of Satan more than the light of God will pay a heavy price for continued evildoings. Those who keep pulling away from Jesus so they can walk in darkness eventually reach the place that there is no more light in them.

CHAPTER 12

Knock, Knock! Who's There?

IS IT OK FOR CHRISTIANS TO KEEP SINNING?

As a minister I sometimes run into opposition from people who think that they can keep on sinning and go to heaven. They believe this because they have not been properly taught about the topics of repentance and obedience. When you talk to them about God's requirement for us to repent and be obedient, they will often quote Scriptures which declare that we are saved by grace through faith in Jesus Christ and not by our own works.

These people have been taught a false gospel and as a result they fail to understand that repentance and obedience are not the same thing as works. They are different things altogether. Repentance and obedience are products of a right attitude toward God. We cannot earn Salvation through repentance and obedience any more than we can earn salvation by performing good works, but repentance and obedience are behavioral evidence that we want to serve God.

Another opposition that happens when you bring up God's requirement for us to repent and remain repentant in order to be saved is the "we are no longer under the law" argument. Again, God's word explains that repentance and the "law" are two different things.

God's requirement for mankind to repent and believe on His promised

Redeemer was in place long before the Law was given to Moses. It has existed ever since the Garden of Eden. Repentance is the call of God's Spirit to turn away from evil. It is God's call to love God and love our fellow man. Jesus said that we are doing well if we do these things. All of the rest of the "Law" was introduced during the time of Moses because of humanity's hard and rebellious hearts. The Law only exists because of man's refusal to repent without God's legislation.

JESUS ADDRESSES UNREPENTANCE IN THE CHURCH

In the book of Revelation Jesus Christ takes almost three whole chapters to address problems that were already beginning to surface in corporate Christianity during the first century of its conception. The book of Revelation was written by the apostle John when he was in exile on the Isle of Patmos near the end of his life ministry.

There are some leaders who have made efforts to suggest that the seven churches represent different denominations. Others teach that the seven churches refer to different stages of the church in history, with the lukewarm Church of Laodicea being the predominant state of Christianity in the last days before Christ's return.

There may be some elements of truth to these comparisons, but we must be careful not to miss the more important teaching that Jesus repeats seven times throughout Chapter 2 and 3 of Revelation:

> Whoever has ears, let them hear what the Spirit says
> to the churches. Revelation 3:22 NIV

Even though Jesus addresses each church individually, He finishes each package of warnings and exhortations with the same phrase (addressing all the churches). Why? Jesus did this because the positive and negative aspects that Jesus was referring to can exist in **any** church. Jesus encourages all of us to continue walking in the Spirit, but He also warning all of us to deal with the unrepentance that exists within our lives.

Those whom I love I rebuke and discipline. So be earnest and repent. Here I am! I stand at the door and knock. If anyone hears my voice and opens the door, I will come in and eat with that person, and they with me. To the one who is victorious, I will give the right to sit with me on my throne, just as I was victorious and sat down with my Father on his throne. Revelation 3:19-21 NIV

Many preachers like to paint the evangelistic picture of Jesus standing at the door of the unbeliever's heart knocking, but that is only a half-truth. Here in the book of Revelation, Jesus is addressing **unrepentant professing Christians** just the same way that he was trying to reach unrepentant, sinful Israel. He is addressing the churches and telling us that He is standing at the door of our hearts politely knocking to be let in.

WE ARE THE FIRST DOOR

Many people have not been properly taught that there are two doors on the path of Salvation. The first is the door of our hearts. Regardless of our profession about being Christian, if we are unrepentant, our heart's door is turned toward darkness leaving Jesus and the Holy Spirit on the outside, knocking to be allowed in. When we choose to repent, our heart is turned towards God's light and Jesus and the Holy Spirit can then enter in. We then have the inner light and the spiritual power necessary to enable us to see the path to salvation and take up our cross to follow Jesus along this path.

Professing Christians think of Jesus knocking at the door of the unbeliever and asking to be let in, but this message from Jesus in the book of Revelation is not a message to the heathen. This message is to the churches. We must hear what the Spirit is saying to every one of the churches in Revelation 3:20 "Behold, I stand at the door and knock. If any man hears my voice and opens the door, I will come in to him and will sup with him, and he with me."

Today, Jesus is standing knocking at the door of the hearts of many professing, backslidden Christians. All throughout the nation of Christianity Jesus is knocking on people's hearts wanting to come in.

Preachers don't do professing Christians any favors by suggesting that we are not sinners, only forgetful and thus not responsible for our continued disobedience.

Our hearts are a door that can only open one way. When we turn our hearts away from God and open our hearts to sinfulness and darkness, we leave Jesus and the Holy Spirit on the outside, continually knocking on the back of our door to be allowed back in. Jesus Christ will not force Himself into our lives. Whether or not He will come in and abide with us is totally dependent upon which way the door to our heart is facing.

When Adam and Eve turned away from God in rebellion and disobedience, the doors of their hearts were turned toward evil and darkness, leaving God on the outside, knocking to get back in. Then when they turned their hearts back towards God, choosing to repent and believe in God's promise of a Redeemer, light came back into their lives because their door was once again facing the Lord. God was able to enter in and fellowship with them again.

The way of Salvation today is exactly the same as it was six thousand years ago. It is only when we turn back to God's light and repent that Jesus is able to come in to our heart and the Holy Spirit is able to heal us and help us to get up and continue on the narrow path of repentance, following Jesus in faith and obedience to Father God.

In the book of Matthew, it is the repentant who are the five wise virgins who have the presence of Jesus and the Holy Spirit within them. It is the repentant who will have the abiding light within them to be able to find the second door, the door of Heaven that the Bridegroom will open for us when He comes. Then that door will be closed and the unrepentant will be left behind to share the fate of the heathen. Sadly, Christ's response to unrepentant professing Christians will be "Depart from me evildoers, workers of iniquity. I do not know you."

Salvation will still be available for all left on Earth at that time, but the door to Heaven for the living will remain closed for seven more years and none will be spared of the horrors of the seven year tribulation as a consequence of their continued unrepentance and disobedience. Don't you understand that God does not want that to happen to any of us?

It took me many years to learn that when we hear the message of the Gospel and turn to God in repentance and faith in Jesus Christ, the door of our heart is facing God. We are facing the grace and mercy and forgiveness of God. The light of God pushes out the darkness in our lives and Jesus can enter in and dwell with us. As long as we determine to continue to face God and progress toward God on the narrow path of repentance and obedience, Jesus and the Holy Spirit will always be there with us to guide and help us to victory.

JESUS IS THE SECOND DOOR, THE ONLY WAY TO SALVATION

The second door that the Bible tells us is necessary for our salvation is Jesus Himself. God wants us to understand that Jesus is the only door that provides entry for the human race to be restored back into God's family.

> Then said Jesus unto them again, Verily, verily, I say unto you *, I am the door of the sheep. All that ever came before me are thieves and robbers: but the sheep did not hear them. I am the door: by me if any man enter in, he shall be saved, and shall go in and out, and find pasture. John 10:7-9 KJV

Jesus is the light that shines in the darkness, but it is the turning of our heart's door away from darkness towards the light (repentance) that enables us to see God's door to heaven. It is also the key to unlocking the doorway to eternal life. We cannot come into God's kingdom through Jesus if we insist on continuing to walk in sin and darkness in the opposite direction to the one that Jesus walks. The only way out of the darkness is to turn toward the light of God and follow Him.

> Jesus spoke to the people once more and said, "I am the light of the world. If you follow me, you won't have to walk in darkness, because you will have the light that leads to life." John 8:12 NLT
>
> Don't let your hearts be troubled. Trust in God, and trust also in me…Jesus told him, "I am the way, the

truth, and the life. No one can come to the Father except through me. John 14:1-6 NLT

I have come as a light to shine in this dark world, so that all who put their trust in me will no longer remain in the dark. I will not judge those who hear me but don't obey me, for I have come to save the world and not to judge it. John 12:46-47 NLT

MY CHAINS ARE GONE!
I'VE BEEN SET FREE!

In the old hymn "Amazing Grace" there is a verse that begins with "My chains are gone, I've been set free". On that day in 1981 as I turned to God in complete repentance, it was like a blindfold of darkness had been ripped away from my eyes and I could finally see the truth. For the first time in my life I suddenly understood what the writer of that song meant.

Just because we have the knowledge of evil within our nature, this does not mean that we have to sin. The truth is that Satan cannot make us sin if we really want to overcome evil and follow Jesus. Satan only offered Adam and Eve three choices. He only offered Jesus three choices. All he ever offers any of us is three choices. He entices us to sin through the pride of life (vanity). He tempts us to sin through lust of the eyes (desire) and urges us to sin through the lust of the flesh (greed), but listen to me. There is another path for us.

God showed me that there is a fourth path for us to follow in life, the path of repentance, the path of trusting in God's Word and walking with Jesus in obedience to God. If we choose to follow Jesus, God promises us that Satan cannot force us to continue sinning. God will enable us through the Holy Spirit to do what He is asking us to do, to overcome and to be victorious over sin.

Trust in the LORD with all your heart; do not depend on your own understanding. Seek his will in all you do, and he will show you which path to take. Proverbs 3:5-6 NLT

GOD SHOWED ME THE PATH

If you doubt that God will be there to show us which paths to take, let me share with you what happened right after I made a commitment to fully repent and obey God with all my heart. When I lifted my head up from the steering wheel at around nine in the morning I had no idea where I was. I had only parked in a random downtown street stall because I was an emotional basket case and couldn't see to drive any more.

I had never been to downtown Williams Lake before. I had only driven through the outskirts of the town on my way to somewhere else. Yet when I lifted my head off the steering wheel and looked at the door right in front of me, I could see that it was a lawyer's office and there was someone inside.

I already knew that if I was going to fully repent and follow God, I would have to return to my home town. I would need to face the consequences of my past sins and try as much as possible to make things right with my wife and children. I knew that this was going to require getting some psychological counselling. Plus I knew I needed legal advice in consideration of the possibility that I could go to jail for some time due to some of the things that I had done. It was not going to be easy but I was now determined to put God's Word to the test.

I got out of the car and tried the door of the lawyer's office. It was locked, so I knocked on the glass until the guy inside answered. When he came to the door all of my pent-up emotions just flooded out again onto this poor fellow as I told him my story, complete with my commitment that I wanted to make God the Lord of my life.

Well, surprise! Surprise! It turned out that this lawyer was a Christian lawyer, a real Christian lawyer, a man who loved God and understood that this was a divine appointment from God. He wasn't open on a Saturday. What lawyer is? He had just felt that it was important for him to come to the office to catch up on some work, and then I showed up.

I don't even remember the man's name. I just remember that he prayed with me. He encouraged me that I was doing the right thing. He gave me some good legal advice. He recommended a psychologist and a lawyer located close to where I lived. Then I headed back to my home town to begin my new life determined that from that day forward I was going to believe God rather than Satan.

Sure, I've stumbled on occasion since then and had to repent and ask God for forgiveness. We all do, but ever since that day, I have tried my best to trust in God rather than in my own understanding. I have done my best to start walking with God in repentance and obedience, rather than the former ways that had ruined my life. I experienced a spiritual birth on that day. I was born again with a desire to truly serve God.

The Word of God says that when we get to that place in our lives, we actually become a new creature through Jesus Christ, and I don't doubt this at all. I have never for one moment ever regretted my decision that day to turn away from evil and truly follow after Jesus Christ.

Some years later when I ran into an old biker buddy from my sinful days and I was sharing with him how God had changed my life, he made the comment that if the person that I am now ran into the person who I was back then, we wouldn't get along at all. He was right. I am no longer the person I once was. I am a different person. I am a new creature in Christ.

I am no longer the drunk who used to smoke weed and throw liquor empties into the parking lots of churches, calling them hypocrites. I am no longer the guy who used to tear past churches revving my motorcycle while church was in session just to annoy the people inside. More importantly, I am longer the person whose life was ruled and controlled by sin and addictions, yet imagined that he was just as good as a lot of professing Christians and better than some.

Now I am the person teaching the way of Salvation to the people both inside the church and outside the church. Today I do my best to bring others to Christ while doing my best to keep my own sinful desires subject to the Lord, conscious of the fact that I do not want to end up a castaway myself after having led others to Jesus.

DON'T EXPECT GOD TO ALWAYS
FIX EVERYTHING THAT WE MESS UP

Over the past thirty-five years since I turned my life over to Jesus I have seen God do some miraculous things in my own life and in the lives of many other people. Nonetheless, God doesn't always make everything go away or return to the way they were before we destroyed it all just because we become Christians, particularly when it involves past sins that we have committed.

On the contrary, there can be long lasting consequences for those who follow evil for a time. Yes, God will always forgive us if we return to Him with a truly repentant heart, but the consequences of a single sinful indiscretion in our lives can continue to have serious repercussions on Earth for generations.

Adam and Eve turned back to God but they still died and we still all die because of their original sin. Their firstborn son still murdered his brother as a result of the sin-nature that Adam and Eve brought into the human race. Both Noah and Lot had problems with drunkenness that brought shame and conflict which extended into their immediate family, and affected future generations as well.

Abraham, David and Solomon all ignored God's instructions not to have more than one wife and the offspring from their indiscretions grew up to become enemies of Israel. In fact, some of their Arab descendants are still enemies of Israel and anyone else who is not Arab to this very day.

David repented of his sin of murder, but God still permitted David's firstborn child from the relationship to die because of the sin, and Absalom, a son by one of his extra wives also became a murderer. In the end Absalom even tried to murder his own father David and take over the throne. Then let's not forget the thief on the cross. Jesus forgave him, but the thief still had to die on the cross that day for the sins that he had committed in the past.

Don't think that becoming a Christian means that the results of all of our past evil behavior will magically vanish and there will be no consequences for any sins that we have committed in the past, or are involved in now, or commit in the future. Any person who has a television knows that there are numerous prominent Christians and Christian ministers throughout the world today whose families, ministries and reputations have been destroyed because of continuing unrepentant sin in their lives.

Continuing sin always has consequences. If you think that you are immune from it, you are only deceiving yourself. I went to Bible College from 1985 to 1987 and many of the students who attended there have seen their lives seriously damaged as a result of unrepentant sin. Some have even died. Even the school itself eventually withered up and died as a result of leadership being too concerned about pleasing man and not enough concerned about pleasing God.

Did God fix everything that I had messed up during my years of disobedience? No! God helped me restore some things, but not everything. I have learned that some bad things that we have done in life can't be undone in spite of our best efforts to make them right. All we can do is to try to do our best to go forward and not make the same mistakes again.

I have also discovered that the consequences of past sins can sometimes come back later on in life and you will have to deal with them. However, if we trust in God and His love, He will always direct our paths and help us deal with whatever comes our way. The Bible is true when it says that if we trust in God, He will work all things together for good.

LIVING WITH THE CONSEQUENCES
OF OUR SIN IS NEVER EASY

Without a doubt, the hardest thing that I had to deal with at that time in my life was my wife's decision for our marriage to not be reconciled. As much as I did not want it to happen, my wife soon moved with our children to another part of Canada and eventually remarried.

I cannot blame my wife or think badly of her for doing this. It was not her evil behavior that had caused our marriage to fail. It was mine. I know that I had just hurt her too deeply and she was unable to trust me anymore or cope with allowing me back into her life and the lives of our children.

I also knew that I had no right to judge my wife for leaving me for another man. Together, we had done almost exactly the same thing to her first husband when I had moved in with her in the beginning while she was still married, so who was I to be the one to point fingers?

Do you remember what I said about having to deal with the consequences of our past sins? I had to come to grips with the truth that (as a result of my own sin) I was now experiencing the same heartache and sorrow that her first husband had suffered when another man (me) came and took away his wife and children. The Word of God says that we reap what we sow, and now I was reaping. It was the most painful lesson of all for me to learn.

I did not want to ever make the same mistakes again. It would be thirteen years and a whole lot of spiritual growth before God opened the door for me to marry again. This time it would be with Jesus and the Holy Spirit at the helm of my life and now twenty-five years later we still love each other as much as when we first married. Yet we both love God more.

CHAPTER 13

Are God's Ways Unjust?

WHAT KIND OF GOD WOULD LET
MURDERERS, RAPISTS, ADULTERERS, PROSTITUTES AND CHILD ABUSERS INTO HEAVEN?

The truth is that God does not allow such people into heaven. God will not allow anyone into heaven who is still walking an evil path when they die. Who deserves to go to heaven, and who does not? The real question on many people's minds is "What kind of God would love and bless people with such an evil past just because they repent, and yet reject me when I have been a decent, hard-working person all my life? It's just not fair!"

People sometimes express offence and indignation at the idea that God could ever love and forgive people who were once great sinners and have now repented. In their minds such people don't deserve to be forgiven. They deserve to be punished for their sins. However, they think that we deserve to be forgiven for OUR sins because we are decent people and our sins are not so bad.

As a matter of fact, it is the sin of pride which is at the forefront in the heart of those who reject God for such reasons. We refuse to admit that we are sinners and in need of salvation when the Word of God clearly states that all have sinned and fall short of God's goodness. How ready we are to judge and condemn others for their sins. Yet how easily we excuse our own wickedness and consider ourselves good enough to make heaven through our own track record.

EVIL IS A DEADLY BLINDING POISON

Jesus and the Apostles ran into this kind of reasoning in their day and obviously the same vain concept of entitlement still exists in our day. People are still denying God's Word. They are still rejecting God and believing the lie that continuing to embrace the knowledge of good and evil will "earn" us a future of becoming like "gods". God's word explains to us that this was the kind of thinking that once led to such a corruption of human society that mankind's every thought became wicked and eventually the whole world had to be destroyed with a flood to give future generations of humanity another chance to follow the truth.

We don't want to believe that it is possible for modern society to eventually become so embedded with evil that there will be no good left in us. We don't want to believe that we could become murderers, yet our present generation is already killing unborn babies by the millions, and there is lobbying going on to kill the infirm and elderly as well. Every day around the world millions more people are dying from violence, neglect, disease and starvation, people who could be helped, but no one helps them. We may not have a hand in it personally, but it is still happening.

The really crazy thing is that this "end times" generation is once again fast headed toward the same levels of violence and immorality that existed in Noah's day but we don't see it. We still want to go our own way. We still want to know good **and** evil. The world still refuses to believe God and turn back to Him in repentance and faith in Jesus Christ.

JESUS DIED FOR ALL

Listen to me, dear reader. Either Jesus Christ has the desire and power to forgive us and cleanse us of every sin, or He does not have the ability to forgive any sin at all. God did not offer up His beloved Son to die on the cross only for your sin or my sin. Jesus Christ suffered and died so that every single sinner in the world who repents and believes on Jesus Christ could be forgiven and come back to Father God.

> For the message of the cross is foolishness to those who are perishing, but to us who are being saved it is the power of God. For it is written: "I will destroy the wisdom of the wise; the intelligence of the intelligent I will frustrate." Where is the wise person? Where is the teacher of the law? Where is the philosopher of this age? Has not God made foolish the wisdom of the world? For since in the wisdom of God the world through its wisdom did not know him, God was pleased through the foolishness of what was preached to save those who believe. Jews demand signs and Greeks look for wisdom, but we preach Christ crucified: a stumbling block to Jews and foolishness to Gentiles, but to those whom God has called, both Jews and Greeks, Christ the power of God and the wisdom of God. 1 Corinthians 1: 18-24 NIV

Don't let this wonderful example of undeserved love become a stumbling block to you. The Apostle Paul explains to us that the religious crowds become offended and the unbelievers think that it is all nonsense when we preach that the death of Jesus Christ paid the price for the redemption of all who repent and believe on Him for Salvation, but it is true.

Have you done your best to serve God all your life? Good for you! God loves you and everything He has is yours to share. But you have to realize that we all start out as God's children and God loves ALL of His children. He loves the ones who have gone to terrible depths of depravity just as much as He loves you. That is why (when they repent) God embraces them and receives them back with love, forgiveness, mercy and great joy.

Even human parents don't abandon their children for disobedience. When a child doesn't listen to their parents' instructions about not running wild in the house and they fall and hurt themselves or break something valuable, their parents may not be happy about it, but they don't stop loving them. When they run away from home and get mixed up in bad stuff, we still love them. We still want them to come to their senses and come back to us. There are even mothers of murderers who still love their child and grieve greatly over the way their child has gone. Do we not realize that God's capacity for love, mercy and forgiveness is far greater than ours?

That is why I know that God has forgiven me now that I have come back to Him. Like the prodigal son in the Bible, I know that, even though I was once guilty of terrible wickedness, God never stopped loving me and looking for me to come back to Him. Now that I am back, I don't ever want to leave again. Why would I ever go back to the Devil, the cruel step-father who destroyed my life and the lives of all of those whom I loved?

CONFESSION AND FORGIVENESS

True Christianity teaches that we must repent of our sins and this sometimes involves confessing our guilt to the ones we have sinned against and doing our best to make reparations to our victims. Under certain circumstances we may also be required to confess our sin to the church as well. For example: a person in leadership who has been involved in illegal or immoral activities may be required to confess and repent of their sin before the body of Christ to testify that such behavior is evil and unacceptable conduct for Christians.

In addition to this, the Word of God instructs that all professing Christians (including leaders) who refuse to repent of following after evil must be confronted by the church. If they still refuse to repent, they must be rejected from fellowship until they change their ways. Sinners may view this as harsh and unloving, but that is because they love their sin more than they love God. They love darkness more than they love those they are sinning against.

SHOULD THE CHURCH PROTECT
THOSE WHO CONTINUE TO DO EVIL?

Such a vile concept should never exist in the church, and yet it does exist in many churches throughout the world today. The idea that an unrepentant person can go into a church and confess their sin to a priest or pastor and be absolved of their guilt without ever truly repenting of their evil is an abomination to the Lord.

Christian ministers who become aware of things like theft, adultery, rape, child abuse, violence and murder and then proceed to cover it up and allow it to continue under the unbiblical philosophy of confidentiality are sinners. They will one day be judged by God for their evil, just as guilty as if they had committed the crime themselves.

The proper conduct for ministers in these situations is to do their best to convince the offender to repent and face the consequences for the evil that they have done. If they refuse to repent, they must be turned over to the authorities to be judged just as you would with any other criminal. Only a fool would think that God will not judge the evil behavior that goes on within some church circles hiding and protected behind perversions of the concepts of confidentiality and sanctuary.

ARE CHRISTIANS ABOVE THE LAW?

Of course not! The law exists to be a terror to all evildoers, including professing Christians. If you think that you can profess Christianity to keep yourself out of jail or use it as a "get out of jail free" card when you are incarcerated, you are only deceiving yourself.

Christianity is not a free ride for evil-doers. God brought the Law into existence because of unrighteousness. The professing Christian who is involved in criminal activities is just as deserving of criminal prosecution as the avowed unbeliever. Don't be confused about the difference between forgiveness and justice.

God forgives the repentant sinner, but that does not mean that we will necessarily be spared from the legal consequences of the law for the sins that we have committed. Jesus forgave the repentant thief on the cross for his life of sin, but the man did not escape his suffering and death for his transgressions.

Why is it that so many professing Christians can imagine the fantasy of being willing to go to jail or suffer for their faith in Jesus, and yet they are abhorred at the idea that they deserve to be in jail for their evil behavior? The Word of God tells us that if we suffer for righteousness sake there is a reward. However, God's Word also tells us that if we suffer for our own faults, if we have done the crime, we deserve to do the time. We should do so without complaining. The Word of God states that governments and laws and police and judges exist to be a terror to those whose hearts are set to follow after wickedness, and professing Christians are not exempt.

WHERE IS THE JUSTICE FOR PAST VICTIMS OF FORMER SINNERS?

Where is justice? Are you offended that God forgives repentant sinners? Why should those who are guilty of horrendous past sins be allowed into heaven? The Word of God does have an answer to these questions, but whether or not it makes sense to you will hinge on what you choose to believe regarding the history and future of the human race.

Are you a person who believes that mankind is nothing more than randomly evolved creatures who originated from pond-slime and sub-apes? Are we beings without design or purpose? Do you believe that human beings will all one day die and cease to exist as the evolutionists teach? If you embrace these false beliefs, they will cloud your comprehension of how God is able to recompense those who innocently suffer during this lifetime.

The Apostle Paul once said that if our fragile natural lifespan is the only thing that mankind has to look forward to, life would be little more than a hopeless and miserable existence for many people. Undeserved suffering covers the entire planet and if this life is all there is, many people would be better off if they had never even been born.

On the other hand, if we choose to believe God's promise that we were all created as eternal spiritual beings who will only live out the first tiny fraction of our eternal lives in these mortal bodies, our perspective on life and the things that we suffer during our natural lifespan will change immensely.

Life on Earth can be cruel at times, but God promises that this present life that we live is less than the blink of an eye in comparison to eternity. God has all eternity to make up for any and all unjust suffering that every human being on Earth endures during their natural lifespan on planet Earth. God promises that one day He is going to erase all pain and sorrow from the hearts of those who love Him. Even the memory of all former evils will be totally forgotten.

When God's love is so unfathomable that He is willing to forgive and pardon the greatest of sinners when they repent, do you not realize that God will be even more motivated to provide love and healing and comfort and eternal compensation to those who have innocently suffered evil during their natural lives on Earth? God is extremely good and His mercy endures forever.

I assure you that God will not fail to heal and reward the suffering of the innocent who have chosen to trust in Him, and He has all eternity to make good for anything people innocently suffer in our mortal lives here on Earth, especially since our entire life on Earth is less than the blink of an eye when compared to eternity.

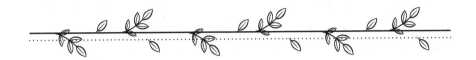

CHAPTER 14

Travelling a New Path

GOD HEALS OLD FAMILY WOUNDS

Some sins just cannot be undone. I prayed for reconciliation, but unfortunately, my marriage was not recoverable and I realized that I had to move on with life. God did help me in many other ways, though. My mother and I had not been close for years. Until that point in my life, I had not treated my mother very well due to deep seated resentments regarding her alcoholism that went all the way back into my early childhood.

In fact, the last memory that I have of my mother before my own life fell apart was the previous March when Mom had phoned to invite us all to Easter dinner. I agreed to come, but warned Mom that we would not stay if she was drinking when we arrived. She promised not to be drunk.

The moment that we pulled into the driveway and she came out to greet us, there was no mistaking the slurred speech and the wobbly stance. Mom was bombed again. I told her we were leaving and never even got out of the car. She grabbed onto the door handle begging me to stay, but I was so angry and my heart was so hard that I continued to back out of the driveway with her holding onto the door handle, dragging her along as I went until she couldn't hold on any longer and fell into the dirt. My children were screaming but I kept on going.

It is now thirty-nine years later and I can still see that picture in my mind. When I reflect on the fact that I had considered myself a Christian at the time, it is evidence of just how deluded I was during that point in my life. On top of all these things, while God was dealing with me in Williams Lake I missed my own step-father's funeral, leaving Mom to deal with everything all by herself when she needed me the most. Yet God had a special way for me to help make up for my past mistreatment of my mother.

A NEW CREATURE IN CHRIST JESUS

I was a different person when I came back from Williams Lake. God had opened my eyes to see that Mom's sins were no worse than my own. I understood now that they were only different from mine and it gave me a love and compassion for my mother that I had never had before. I told Mom everything that had happened to cause the breakup of my marriage and how sorry I was for the way I had been treating her and for not being there to support her at Dad's funeral. I told her all about my encounter with God in Williams Lake and that I was now determined to truly live for God for the rest of my life.

The end result was that although Mom was somewhat shocked and a little skeptical about everything that I said to her, she told me that she had been struggling with her own depression and loneliness now that Dad was gone. Mom offered to let me stay with her until I could find a place of my own as long as I didn't start preaching to her.

I laughed about that and agreed to her terms. I didn't have to preach to her. It was the start of a reconciliation between myself and my mother that would culminate with her badly wanting what I now had. In her own time, Mom too accepted Jesus as her Savior and was delivered from her own addictions. Our last dozen years together before she went to be with Jesus would finally become the loving family relationship that had long been missing from both of our lives.

Years afterward when we talked about that first day, Mom said that she wasn't sure at first whether or not I had gone over the deep end, but she knew something was definitely different about me when I came back. I knew that too. Finally I knew what it was to be born again with God as my Father.

MANY FACES OF
CHRISTIAN CHARITY

One thing that I learned during that period of my life is that true Christian charity has nothing to do with what group or denomination you belong to. Whereas years ago Mom had encountered professing Christians who were unwilling even to bury her dead, this time around both church and community stepped up to help a grieving low-income pensioner in need.

Some people are fortunate enough to have a financial nest-egg when someone dies, but Dad's insurance company had gone bankrupt a year before he passed away. Instead of an inheritance of some kind, the only thing Dad's sinful lifestyle had left Mom with was six months back rent that had accumulated against their rented home while Dad was in the hospital. Financially things were not good, but God saw her need and had mercy on her.

I found out after my return to our home town that (since my step-father was an ex-serviceman) the local Legion had graciously covered Dad's funeral costs. Also, the United Church minister had heard of her plight and volunteered to perform the funeral service for Mom. In addition, the rental home that Mom and Dad had been living in was owned by the company that Dad was working for when he became ill. It was a relief that they were compassionate enough to cancel the back rent debt when he passed away

As for me, upon returning home I was not comfortable going to my former minister for counsel since his wife had gained a reputation for sharing the intimate details of parishioners' lives with others. Therefore, I approached the pastor of another local church and found him to be a kind and devout man who was a great help to me. He agreed to counsel me whenever I felt that I needed someone to talk to even though I continued attending another church of a different denomination because of my core beliefs.

At the time of my marital breakup, I was completely broke, worse than broke. I was deeply in debt with no money, no assets, no job and no transportation, but my thinking had changed, and I now knew that if I did the right thing, God would take care of my own needs. God did so, but it didn't happen overnight.

GOD BEGINS TO
OPEN DOORS FOR ME

The local lumber economy was still in a nose dive and I was not expecting much success at job hunting. When I went to apply at the local sawmill where I had worked years before, I was surprised when the hiring person recognized me. He turned out to be someone who had been a good friend of my step-father. In spite of the economy slump I was hired immediately to go back to the well-paying lumber grading job that I had left years before. I was forced to hitch hike to work for the first few paychecks, but soon I had saved six hundred dollars to purchase a decent used sedan.

The pastor of the local Pentecostal Church offered to let me rent a one bedroom cabin that been the former pastorate, charging me only a very nominal rent. After talking things over with Mom and determining that she was going to be alright living on her own now, I moved into my own place.

I was overjoyed when a friend gave me a little grey kitten as a housewarming gift At least I would have something to keep me company as I continued to mourn the loss of my wife and children from my life. Things were starting to improve, but you never know when there might be more heartache coming in your life. It could be just around the corner.

GOD'S MERCY IN THE FORM OF
A TORTOISE SHELL CAT

If anyone ever tries to tell you that becoming a Christian is all good times, lollipops and rainbows they are mistaken. God does some wonderful things in the lives of believers, but that does not mean that there will be no more trials and tribulations in our lives. God never promised that this life would always be fair or pleasant. What He does promise is that if we trust in Him, He will help us get through whatever adversities come our way.

My first setback occurred only a few days after I had moved into my cabin. I woke up in the morning to find that the beautiful little kitten that I had been given was dead in his bed. It crushed me. It tore my heart out. I wailed and suffered over the death of that little creature just as much as I had over my own family leaving. As I went through this grief, Satan the accuser was telling me how worthless and terrible I was. I could not keep a wife. I could not take care of my children. What kind of person, what kind of Christian was I that couldn't even care for a kitten without killing it?

The whole thing was devastating to me, but after a long hard cry I calmed down enough to come back to trusting in God and rejecting Satan's attacks. The truth was that this was just one of those things that happen in life and we have no explanation for it. If anyone killed the kitten, it was Satan, not me and not God. Satan is after all the angel who has the power of death. God reminded me that it was OK to mourn for the kitten, but I was not responsible for its death.

Eventually I regained my composure enough that I decided to go and sit in the sun on the front steps. It was a beautiful warm day and as I was sitting there soaking in the sun's warmth, a full-grown tortoise shell cat came up and started rubbing against me and purring. This comforted me a lot. It was like God was saying to me that everything was going to be OK, so we just sat there enjoying each other's company for quite a while.

When I got up to go back into the house, the cat waltzed right in and made herself at home. For the next four years this cat would become my constant companion and comforter. She followed me everywhere, even when I went on hikes through the fields. She remained with me until I was well into my second year at Bible College and strong enough to make it on my own. Then one day I let her out to go to the bathroom and she just disappeared and I never saw her again. I missed the cat after that, but I knew I was going to be able to make it on my own by then. Thank you Jesus for a tortoise shell cat.

Michael Hunter

LEARNING TO TRUST GOD

In the beginning I had no vehicle so I had to hitchhike to work, but as I already said, after a couple of months I had managed to scrape together six hundred dollars to buy a decent used car. I was really happy to have reliable transportation again. I greatly appreciated that car and it was important to me. There was no bus service in our town and my work was about five miles from where I lived. If you could not car-pool with someone, the only other viable alternative was hitch-hiking or walking.

Everything was good until I arrived at church one Sunday afternoon and there was a widow in the congregation whose car had broken down and was unfixable. Since she lived out of town and had small children, an appeal was made to the congregation for anyone who had an extra car that she would be able to borrow until the family could afford to get another one. Right away, I heard God say "Give her the car!"

In a fine example of my spiritual generosity and maturity, my first response was "God, I don't want to have to hitch hike again". So I waited for someone else to step up and volunteer something, but no one else did and the Lord repeated Himself again, adding "Who do you love more, Me or the car? Do you love the woman, or the car? Give her the car?"

That was enough for me. I handed the keys to her explaining that I felt that God wanted me to give the car to her and she was very grateful. It felt good, regardless of the inconvenience that it was going to be for me to have to hitch hike again until I could afford another car. A short time later, we signed the papers and I was back to walking again.

I was fully prepared to have to go back to hitch hiking to work for quite a while until I could afford another car, but later that week I happened to be walking past the GM dealership and I noticed that they were loading vehicles onto one of those car-hauling trailers. I spotted a near new Datsun pickup in the line waiting to be loaded and felt led by the Lord to stop and ask them about the truck. The owner of the dealership told me that they had not been able to move the vehicle so it was on its way to another location.

Then he asked me if I was interested and he offered me a very good below market price. I explained to him that I appreciated his offer and really liked the truck but had just gotten back to work. I did not have the

94

cash and was pretty sure that I would be unable to get financing for it. The owner took me into his office. He sold me the truck on the spot and took care of the financing himself at a very reasonable rate. So the end result of it all was that I had given my 20 year old six hundred dollar car to God and He had replaced it with a nice pickup less than 2 years old at a very reasonable price and low payments. Listening to God had turned out to be not that bad a decision after all. I got a lot of work and miles out of that truck.

GOD PROVIDES WOOD

I have experienced many examples of God's provision over the years since then, but another one that stands out during those early days of serving God involved a middle aged godly Christian woman whose husband had abandoned her. She was unable to work because of poor health and was living in a terrible little shack in the middle of town. Her only sources of heat and cooking were two old wood stoves in a climate that could reach forty below zero in the winter time.

To make matters worse, the roof leaked like a sieve when it rained and the landlord refused to do anything about fixing the old tar paper roofing over the house. After visiting her one rainy day and seeing the pots scattered around the kitchen to catch the water as it was coming through the holes in the roof, God impressed upon me to help the woman.

Winter was coming on, so firewood was the first priority. All of my extra money was going to pay down my debt load so I didn't have the money to buy firewood for her, but I had a chainsaw and a splitting axe so I prayed to God that if He would help me get the wood, I would split and stack enough to get her through the winter. After all, I now had a nice new pickup to haul it in.

Sometimes I would come across a fallen tree in the bush and cut it up. More often than not during that winter I was simply able to find wood in the form of fence posts or pre-cut firewood that people had left at the dump. There were other times that people who had heard about her need would give wood to me and all I had to do was simply haul it to her house.

Before winter was over, the Lord had helped me provide over twenty cords of wood for her, enough for the coming winter and the next one. For those of you who don't know what a cord is, a single cord is a stack of wood 4 ft. high by 4 ft. wide by 8 ft. long. God really came through big time.

GOD PROVIDES A ROOF

Although I felt good about being able to provide wood for the woman, a new roof was a whole other matter. One of the local churches had offered to donate some tar and roofing nails to the cause if they were needed, but roofing materials and labor are expensive and extra money was one thing that I did not have. I had made a commitment to the Lord to pay off the thirty thousand dollar debt from my business collapse that was still owed to creditors. All of my spare money was being put toward paying down that debt, but God had another way to solve the problem.

One day as I was up at the dump disposing of refuse and looking for firewood, something unusual caught my eye. It was 4 large rolls about 4 feet wide and 3 feet around. When I got closer I could see that these were rolls of used rubber conveyor belting that someone had discarded, **waterproof** rolls. Right away I knew that I had my roofing material for the old shack.

The next problem was to figure out how to get them in the truck by myself. I did not want to go for help in case the city caterpillar machine showed up and pushed them over the bank when I was gone. However, each roll was about three feet by four feet, weighed hundreds of pounds and I had no one to help me. After a lot of prayer, muscle and improvised levers I finally got them all into the truck. Then I contacted some men from our church to come and help put the roofing up.

The guys were astounded that I had managed to get the conveyor belting into the truck by myself. It had to have been with God's help because afterwards it took three of us to get each roll out of the truck. Fortunately the shack was quite small and the conveyor belting was long enough to go over the peak of the roof and down to the eaves on both sides of the house. All we had to do was slit it in the middle to bend over the peak and seal the seams between the belts with tar and roofing nails.

Then when we got down to our last piece, we ran out of nails and not one of us had enough money to buy any more, but God knew how to take care of that problem too. While we were trying to figure out what to do next, one of the non-Christians that I knew from work recognized me as he was walking by.

The man asked what we were up to. I explained to him what we were doing and our dilemma of now being out of roofing nails and not having any money to buy any. "I can take care of that" he said and about ten minutes later he came back with enough nails from the hardware store to finish the job.

Thank you Jesus. After the next rainstorm, the lady was elated to report that there were no more leaks. I would venture to say that, in the end, the roof covering that we installed probably outlasted the rest of that dilapidated old shack. Sometimes God works in mysterious ways, but He still knows how to get the job done.

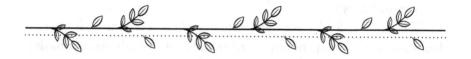

CHAPTER 15

Assembling Together

SMALL CHURCH, BIG VISION.

God's Word says that Christians should not forsake regularly gathering together for fellowship, worship, teaching and prayer, so another thing that I did after returning home was commit to regular church attendance, Bible reading and prayer, and I do mean commit. On Wednesday night, Sunday morning and Sunday evening I went back to attending the church that I had previously frequented, but I wanted more than this.

During the years prior to my own crisis I had crossed paths a few times with members of another small church. They had struck me as a little fanatical at the time because of their joyful exuberance and boldness about sharing Jesus with others. Now I was interested in what they had to say, so I started attending their church as well. It all worked out perfectly because they met on Sunday afternoons, Tuesday evenings and Saturday nights.

If you think that six church services a week is way too excessive, try to understand that up until that period in my life, my time had been filled with family, porn, drugs, booze and other assorted sinful behavior and now it was all gone. There was a huge hole in my life. I wanted to keep in constant contact and fellowship with God's people and His presence until I was strong enough to stand on my own two feet.

I never found it a burden. It was like water to my soul and bread to my spirit. I needed the teaching and the fellowship at the time and I thrived on it for the first two years after coming to Jesus. It was certainly much better than sitting in my cabin alone or getting caught up again in all the things that had gotten me into trouble in the first place.

Let me tell you a little about the two churches that I was attending. The first had started out in a tiny building with a pastor who had a vision of ministering to the city by contacting everyone in town and offering to send a bus around to pick up their children and bring them to Sunday school. Every Sunday morning the bus would be sent out to bring kids to Sunday school and then back home again afterward.

God was behind the idea. Before long, they had to build a bigger church, a much bigger church because many of the parents of the children had begun attending as well as the children. The church continued to thrive and grow for several years. Then something happened that happens in many denominational churches.

Someone up the ladder decided to send this successful pastor and his wife off to try to resurrect another struggling church in different city. They were replaced by a pastor who did not know the people and had little idea of the vision upon which the local assembly was founded. The older replacement pastor had the education and the experience, but he did not have the anointing that the former pastor had.

People began to lose interest and attendance was waning by the time I started to attend regularly. Even though it was theoretically a charismatic church, the services were often lacking in spirit. They were somewhat dry and lifeless. I continued to attend there more out of loyalty to the denomination and loyalty to God than out of actually enjoying and growing from the teaching I was getting there. I was looking for something more out of Christianity than this, but there were still numerous devoted Christians who attended there with whom I became good friends over the years.

Then there was the other church. They were seen as real radicals because they would go around town handing out tracts and talking to people about repentance and Jesus. The senior pastor was also a woman and that is something that is frowned upon by more than a few Christian denominations.

Others even referred to them as a cult, although that was not the impression that I had gotten from previous encounters with them. To me they had seemed like genuine Christians. I was determined that I was going to check them out, so I started attending there as well.

SMALL CHURCH, BIG ANOINTING

Ironically, this was the group that had moved into the small building that the first church had abandoned when they moved into their larger facilities. The meetings of this group were a whole different brand of Christianity. These people were on fire for God. God's love, joy and peace were evident in every service and in the way they greeted and treated people with love and kindness regardless of age, gender, race or social standing.

I doubt if the place seated more than fifty people. I remember that the average service had about thirty people or less in attendance and that was enough to fill the building pretty tightly. When the praise and worship team was called up, almost a third of the congregation went up to the front to minister in music and song to lead the rest of the people.

The congregation wasn't shy about joining in when it was time to worship either. Nobody seemed to be all that concerned about singing talent. Vanity was set aside and everybody was encouraged to participate. Whether people could hold a tune or not didn't seem to matter to anybody. It was liberating. It was definitely a lively, joyful and prayerful place of worship.

The services were planned and orderly but not so rigid that there was no allowance for God to guide the direction and spirit of the meetings. The congregation was encouraged to participate and contribute input as they felt God leading them, all under the guidance, leadership and authority of the pastor and elders. Usually, but not always, the meetings would follow the planned schedule and there would be a snack and beverages afterwards.

Sometimes there would be such a presence of God in the service that the praise and worship of God would continue for most of the meeting and would include spontaneous, unrehearsed praise and prayer from some of those in attendance. Occasionally the praise, worship and prayer would continue for so long that the pastor would just pray for people at the end and promise to preach their message during the next service. It was beautiful that they allowed the Holy Spirit to flow so freely.

I soon found out that these people really knew how to pray. They didn't pray prayers from a book. They prayed to God, not to anybody else listening. They prayed with purpose, abandonment and faith that their prayers would be answered, and let me tell you, some pretty miraculous things happened while I was attending that little church.

Furthermore, their preaching and teaching was solid, Biblical, supported by the Word of God. This little church put spiritual milk in my stomach and spiritual meat on my dry bones that helped me grow quickly. They were also my first real exposure to what the Bible refers to as the Baptism of the Holy Spirit and speaking in tongues. I had heard about it before, but didn't really understand what it was until I started attending there.

They provided good balanced teaching from the Word of God to help me understand that the gifts and ministry of the Holy Spirit are still available and valuable to Christians today. It was something that I definitely wanted in my life and eventually God granted my desire to have all that the Spirit of God wanted to give me.

I was actually quite content to continue to attend and learn from both churches. I saw no harm in it. As far as I was concerned, we were all Christians. However, about two years after accepting Christ, the pastor of the larger church suggested that I shouldn't be dividing my loyalties between two different churches. So I took his advice and stopped going to his church, much to his surprise I am sure. From that time on, I remained a faithful member of the smaller church for several years until I moved with their blessing to another city to attend Bible College.

CHAPTER 16

Modern Miracles?

GOD IS A GOD OF THE IMPOSSIBLE

There are many in the world and in the church today who have trouble believing that God still performs healings and miracles in our day and age, but He certainly does. I can tell you what the Bible has to say about the subject:

> Later Jesus appeared to the Eleven as they were eating; he rebuked them for their lack of faith and their stubborn refusal to believe those who had seen him after he had risen. He said to them, "Go into all the world and preach the gospel to all creation. Whoever believes and is baptized will be saved, but whoever does not believe will be condemned. And these signs will accompany those who believe: In my name they will drive out demons; they will speak in new tongues; they will pick up snakes with their hands; and when they drink deadly poison, it will not hurt them at all; they will place their hands on sick people, and they will get well." After the Lord Jesus had spoken to them, he was taken up into heaven and he sat at the right hand of God. Then the disciples went out and preached everywhere, and the Lord worked with them

and confirmed his word by the signs that accompanied it. Mark 16:14-20 NIV

Once when he was eating with them, he commanded them, "Do not leave Jerusalem until the Father sends you the gift he promised, as I told you before. John baptized with water, but in just a few days you will be baptized with the Holy Spirit." So when the apostles were with Jesus, they kept asking him, "Lord, has the time come for you to free Israel and restore our kingdom?" He replied, "The Father alone has the authority to set those dates and times, and they are not for you to know. But you will receive power when the Holy Spirit comes upon you. And you will be my witnesses, telling people about me everywhere—in Jerusalem, throughout Judea, in Samaria, and to the ends of the earth." After saying this, he was taken up into a cloud while they were watching, and they could no longer see him. Acts 1:4-9 NLT

This is a great passage describing God's promise to move through Christians in miraculous ways. As I continued studying through the New Testament about the accounts of Peter and Stephen and Philip and Paul and John all moving in the realm of the gifts and power of the Holy Spirit, I began to question the arguments of those who claim that God no longer wants to move in this way through Christians.

I began to wonder if God maybe does continue to move in these ways in the lives of those who choose to believe that God will do this. I began to believe that God wanted to move this way in my own life. As I began to ask God to do such things and believed that God will do what He says He will do, I began to also experience the truth that the Holy Spirit and His gifts are still available to us after all.

GOD STILL RESPONDS TO FAITH

Jesus made a couple of remarkable statements to His disciples during His time on Earth:

"I tell you the truth, anyone who believes in me will do the same works I have done, and even greater works, because I am going to be with the Father. You can ask for anything in my name, and I will do it, so that the Son can bring glory to the Father. Yes, ask me for anything in my name, and I will do it! "If you love me, obey my commandments. And I will ask the Father, and he will give you another Advocate, who will never leave you. He is the Holy Spirit, who leads into all truth. The world cannot receive him, because it isn't looking for him and doesn't recognize him. But you know him, because he lives with you now and later will be in you. John 14:12-17 NLT

Jesus replied, "Truly I tell you, if you have faith and do not doubt, not only can you do what was done to the fig tree, but also you can say to this mountain, 'Go, throw yourself into the sea,' and it will be done. If you believe, you will receive whatever you ask for in prayer."
Matthew 21:21-22 NIV

These Biblical passages in the Gospels and Acts bring us to the following questions. Can the Word of God be trusted? Is the Word of God true or not true? Is there any evidence to suggest that God still moves in these ways today? Well, yes there is!

In addition to studying the Bible itself, during this period of my life I also spent a considerable amount of time reading books about some of the pioneers of the Christian faith in North America and elsewhere. I learned about people like the Wesley brothers and Jonathan Edwards and Charles Finney and Smith Wigglesworth and A.A. Alan and Aimee Semple McPherson and Katherine Kuhlman and numerous others who all told of wonderful examples of God moving in miraculous power in response to prayer.

Then amongst my own generation there were those who were on TV at the time who were also proclaiming that God still moves in the miraculous in our generation. Ministers like Oral Roberts, Joel Osteen, Jimmy Swaggart, Jim and Tammy Bakker, John Hagee, Benny Hinn, Peter

Popoff, Rex Humbard, Ernest Angley, Marilyn Hickey, Joyce Meyer, Paula White and the list goes on and on.

Before you object to some of the people that I have included in the above list and complain about some of those whom I may have left out, listen to what the Word of God has to say about God's gifts and calling:

> God's gifts and God's call are under full warranty - never canceled, never rescinded. There was a time not so long ago when you were on the outs with God. But then the Jews slammed the door on him and things opened up for you. Now they are on the outs. But with the door held wide open for you, they have a way back in. In one way or another, God makes sure that we all experience what it means to be outside so that he can personally open the door and welcome us back in. Romans 11:29-32 MSG

I'm sorry if I may have left out some of your favorites. I am sure that many other ministries have testimonies of God moving in miraculous power just as He did in the time of the first Apostles. In addition, some of the men and women of God that I did mention have had serious ethical and moral failures in some areas of their lives and suffered serious repercussions for their sin, but that does not repudiate the promises of God about what He is willing to do when people have faith to believe His Word in a particular area of faith.

God responds to stepping out in faith, regardless of the fact that we as human beings are not perfect and prone to stumbling. All throughout the Bible we have examples of God greatly using people who were flawed and imperfect. Some were guilty of serious sin, yet God still used them in proportion to the faith that they had to believe particular promises of God.

Samson was a perfect example of someone whom God used for a time to perform mighty deeds even though His personal moral life was a mess. In the end Samson paid with his freedom and his life for his sins, but he was still able to move in the power of God for a time in the area that he had faith to believe the promises of God. Then at the end when Samson repented, God heard his prayer and used Samson mightily one last time before he died.

WE MUST NOT BE HELD BACK
BY OUR OWN VANITY

The greatest stumbling blocks to believing that God still moves in signs and wonders today are vanity and self-righteousness. I hear people point to the imperfections and failures in the lives of some of these ministers and declare "See, I told you that it was all of the Devil."

This kind of attitude is not of God. If we allow ourselves to be led astray by our own vanities and perceptions of being better than others, we will become distracted and offended when God uses other people whom we perceive to be flawed and imperfect.

I have news for you. We are all flawed and imperfect! If our faith is in men or women and we focus on human performances we will always end up disappointed and doubting God. When some of the greatest Televangelists were found out to have human flaws just like the rest of us, there were many people who then rejected everything about Christian teachings and turned away from God.

All of their faith had been tied up in the leaders. They had elevated the ministers and ministries into God's place. Then they were devastated when they discovered that these people were only human, subject to the same temptations and failures as the rest of us.

The truth is that God does not use people because they are flawless, but because they have faith to believe the Lord. When we are willing to step out in faith God promises to honor that faith. When some of the largest Televangelists were knocked from their pedestals, it did not destroy my faith in God's Word. It confirmed to me that what God had told me was true. God expects us to repent. If we don't repent, there will be a price to pay for continued evil doing.

When the hidden sins of some of the televangelists exploded onto TV and the pages of the tabloid newspapers it did not destroy my faith because my faith was not in the evangelists. It inspired me to write a Christian tract. The tract warned myself and all others to make sure that we do not retain areas of unrepentance in our lives after we come to Jesus because we cannot have one foot in Christianity and one foot in unrepentance and not have our world collapse around us.

I presented the tract to one of the largest tract publishers in Canada and they saw the merit in the message. They published it for free and since that day tens of thousands of those tracts have been distributed around the world. I have no way of knowing how many people were influenced by that little tract, but I know it was the truth and God was in it.

Before we start throwing stones at other people, we need to look at our own lives. When Christian ministers and ministries fail, we shouldn't be throwing rocks at them. We should be praying that God will bring them to repentance.

Neither should it destroy our faith in God's Word when prominent people stumble. It should serve as a warning to us to take a good look at our own lives and heed the Apostle Paul's message to himself and every other professing Christian:

> So I run with purpose in every step. I am not just shadowboxing. I discipline my body like an athlete, training it to do what it should. Otherwise, I fear that after preaching to others I myself might be disqualified.
> 1 Corinthians 9:26-27 NLT

Paul's message is clear. Don't get so caught up in preaching to others that we forget that we must keep our own thoughts, words and actions disciplined to serve Jesus. It is not enough to proclaim that "Jesus is Lord." None of us wants to be in the position where we are one day crying out to Jesus to open the door and let us in, only to hear Jesus say, "Sorry, you are disqualified, cheater. Depart from me, evildoers and workers of iniquity."

My greatest desire is for every unbeliever who reads this book to become a Christian and for every professing Christian who reads this book to start really trusting that God truly loves us and has our best interests in mind when He commands us to "Go and sin no more".

CHAPTER 17

God is Still Alive

SIGNS AND WONDERS, ARE THEY
ALL FAKE, OR IS SOME OF IT REAL?

I wanted to know. Does God still move in this way today? My first exposure to such things actually happened during the early seventies before I truly repented. One of the things that motivated me to learn more about God's healing power was that my first wife's father was a professing Christian who loved to watch a famous healing televangelist.

After seeing the program at his house, I soon become a regular viewer of the services at home. I was fascinated and sometimes brought to tears by the programs showing adults and children being healed. I used to wonder and hope that this could possibly be genuine and not just more of the charlatanism that was being exposed as occurring in some Christian ministries at the time.

Then my father-in-law became the victim of a rapidly advancing stomach cancer. He was dying in constant agony and the doctors could do little to help him. At the time, I was still walking in disobedience to God. I was not at all ready to completely repent and obey God in my own life, but I was stirred to have compassion for this man whom I cared for.

When I heard on the TV program that it was possible to go to the man of God and be prayed for "in proxy" for someone else's needs, I felt that if there was any chance at all that this would help my father-in-law, it was important for me to go and try this for him. Who knows? Maybe it could help.

If you are unfamiliar with the term "in proxy", it means that you go to a believer for prayer, not for yourself, but for someone else's needs. The man or woman of God then prays for that person's need, laying their hands on you to transfer the power of God into you. Then you return to lay hands on the ailing person and pray for their need, trusting in God to minister to their need. It seemed surreal at the time, but I felt I had to try.

HOPING FOR THE POWER OF GOD

I was honestly desiring to help my father-in-law, but I was also seriously searching for something to convince me that the power of God was still present in the world today. This was not a small venture for me. Even though I was not a true believer yet, I was a sincere seeker of God. My quest would require a 4,000 kilometer flight to the Eastern United States to visit the home church of a minister whom I had only ever seen on television. This was a big deal.

As far as the preacher goes, his name is unimportant and there was nothing about the man's appearance that would draw you to him. He did not have the classic he-man handsomeness that many TV ministers have. He was short, a little overweight and had a rather comical squeaky voice, but there was something about the book that he had written and his TV show suggested to me that this was a man who did his best to walk with God.

I showed up an hour early to make sure that I got a good seat for the service. I was quite surprised to find that this only put me fairly close to the front of what would turn out to be a very long line up just to get into the church. It was a huge building compared to what I was used to seeing. The building was capable of holding a few thousand people and the seating consisted of long wooden pews that could seat twenty or more people per row with perhaps four or five aisles between the rows. An hour later I settled myself into a center pew a few rows from the front and waited for the service to start.

Right from the time that the service began, the air was charged with spiritual energy and an air of expectation from many of those who were in attendance. The praise and worship flowed like water rising and falling in a wonderful way for quite a while until it was time for the announcements, offering and the message of the day. The sermon was centered on repentance, faith in Jesus Christ and the Scriptural promise that God is the same yesterday, today and forever.

Soon the main message was over and then the invitation was given for prayer. The minister encouraged everyone else to remain respectful, reverent and prayerful for the needs of those being ministered to. A few people left right after the sermon, but most stayed and I could see that many were praying fervently.

The front rows had been reserved for those with crutches, wheelchairs and other special needs, so these were first to be prayed for, but they were soon joined by other people streaming to the front from every aisle. Sometimes the minister would stop what he was doing and go out into the middle of the congregation to pray for a particular person. For the first few minutes nothing at all unusual happened, but then the Holy Spirit began to move and things started to happen.

EXPERIENCING THE POWER OF GOD

At first the man of God just continued to be faithful to pray for people without any apparent results. Some fell to the floor and lay there for a while and others simply returned quietly to their seats after being prayed for and that was it.

Then one young couple brought their preschool daughter forward explaining that she was deaf and dumb and had not spoken since birth. The minister put his fingers in the child's ears and commanded the deaf and dumb spirit to come out of the girl and never bother her again. Then he leaned over and spoke into the girl's ear the word "baby" and the child repeated the word. Then he spoke into the other ear and the child said it again. Then he stood behind the girl where she could not see him and said the word again.

The child jumped up and down and clapped her hands as she said "baby" one more time and the child's parents were immediately overcome with years of pent-up emotion as they realized what had just happened. I could tell by the reaction of the child and the parents that this was not trickery. This little girl had been supernaturally healed. This was real. The whole congregation started shouting and praising God as the minister continued to pray for other people; but that was only the beginning. There was more to come.

Soon others began to be healed. Blind people were seeing. Others who were deaf and dumb were praising God. Crutches were being thrown down and people who obviously had not even had the power to stand for years were getting up out of their wheelchairs, first walking and then running around the place. It was glorious.

GOD TOUCHES ME

There was one thing that bothered me about all this. Sometimes during prayer the minister would warn someone to repent of ongoing sin in their life. That frightened me because I knew that my life was not right before God. I wanted to go forward for prayer but I was too afraid of being exposed in front of everybody as a sinner to go forward to the altar. Yet I also desperately wanted to believe in and hear from God.

I was praying with all my might that God would speak to me and help me believe in Him. I also prayed that God would have mercy on my father-in-law and use me to pray for him. I had my eyes closed as tight as I could and was praying with such intensity that I could feel myself literally shaking. Gradually, I began to realize that it was not just me that was shaking. I could hear a loud and powerful rattling noise.

Most of the congregation had been standing during the prayer time. I was also standing at the end seat and I had been holding on to the pew in front of me for support all the time I was praying. When I opened my eyes, I could see the people around me looking at me and the pew that I was holding onto.

No one else was touching the pew and the entire pew was vibrating and rattling up and down in a way that was not humanly possible for me do to a heavy twenty foot wooden bench simply by leaning on it as I prayed. In the corner of my eye, I saw the minister coming toward me and the only thing that he said was "receive what you have been praying for" as he very lightly touched me on the forehead.

Now before I tell you what happened next, let me tell you what didn't happen. I have been to more than a few church meetings in my life where some minister is determined to push people over using their own physical force and claim that it was God. I never want any part of that.

This was different. The man barely touched me and there was a bright light and a loud noise almost like thunder or an electrical discharge only it didn't hurt at all. It was magnificent. Both of my feet left the ground at the same time and I fell helplessly back onto the pew. I lay there unable to move as the love and mercy and peace of God washed over me again and again in wave after wave as I lay there crying while everyone else ignored me and the service went on.

EXPERIENCING MIRACLES DOES NOT ALWAYS MEAN THAT REPENTANCE AND SALVATION HAS OCCURRED

Eventually, I managed to pull myself together enough to enjoy the rest of the service, but after that, everything else seemed anti-climactic, more normal and believable. Then it was all over and I returned back to Canada.

By the time I arrived back at my father-in-law's place, the doctors (at his own request) had basically sent him home to die amongst his family and he was still in great pain. First I told him about all the things that I saw and the things that had happened to me. He encouraged me to pray for him and I laid my hands on his stomach and prayed for God to touch him.

I have seen stranger things since that time, but what followed next was really weird and creepy for someone like myself who had never experienced it before. There was visible movement within my father-in-law's stomach like the movement that you see within the belly of a pregnant woman when the baby kicks or moves against her tummy and this continued for several minutes while I was praying. Then the movement stopped and my father-in-law said immediately that the terrible pain that he had been experiencing was now completely gone.

No, God did not completely heal my father-in-law of cancer that day. I don't know why. Perhaps it was his time to go. What I do know is that God had mercy on him and took the pain away. Right to the end, he thanked me for praying and said that he had no more pain, and to me that was still a miracle.

God does not always answer prayer the way that we think He will or the way that we want Him to, but I believe that God sometimes answers sincere and fervent prayers of people, even when their lives are still messed up and they are not yet where He wants us to be spiritually.

So, does experiencing signs and wonders and miracles save people? Not necessarily. It encouraged me to continue to seek after God but it didn't save me. I still returned to my wicked ways as do many other people, and this unrepentance would cost me greatly later on in life. I implore you not to focus on looking for signs and wonders before you will repent and obey God. Jesus had this to say about those who want to see signs and wonders before they will believe in Him:

> Then some of the Pharisees and teachers of the law said to him, "Teacher, we want to see a sign from you." He answered, "A wicked and adulterous generation asks for a sign! But none will be given it except the sign of the prophet Jonah. Matthew 12:38-39 NIV

The life, and the three and a half year ministry of Jesus was absolutely overflowing with signs and wonders and miracles. Crowds of thousands would come to hear Him preach and when they brought their sick and demonized to Jesus, there were occasions when HE HEALED THEM ALL. In fact, the Word of God tells us that all the wonderful things that He did would have filled volumes if it had all been recorded, but the wicked still demanded to see more before they would believe. They even wanted to put Him to death for healing people on the Sabbath day. Then Jesus said that the only sign that He would give them was that after they had put Him to death, He would rise on the third day.

Even that was not enough of a miracle for some. Many still refused to believe the truth after Christ's Resurrection occurred. So obviously, seeing signs and wonders are not enough to convince some people. On the other hand, just because experiencing signs and wonders are no guarantee of salvation, this does not mean that signs and wonders have ceased, or that they have no value in our modern society.

For one thing, signs and wonders show that God is still a God of love, compassion and mercy, even to sinners. He still wants to heal and deliver us. He still wants to use miracles to get our attention so that we will listen to His call to us to repent, go and sin no more, and believe in Jesus Christ for salvation. The truth is that the Holy Spirit and His gifts are an important part of Christianity, just as important today as they were two thousand years ago.

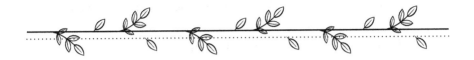

CHAPTER 18

Signs, Wonders and Gifts

SIGNS AND WONDERS
DO NOT SAVE US

Listen to me. Don't focus on the signs and wonders thinking that if you have seen or experienced healings or deliverances or miracles this means that you are automatically going to heaven even if you are continuing to walk in deliberate wickedness. In one place Jesus warned the healed to go and sin no more lest a worse thing come upon them.

Jesus also warned those who were delivered from demons to repent lest the demons return and bring even more wicked ones with them. Jesus Himself marveled that unbelief and disobedience were so deeply entrenched in the lives of people that many had a lot of difficulty believing God's Word without seeing signs to confirm it:

> ...There was a government official in nearby Capernaum whose son was very sick. When he heard that Jesus had come from Judea to Galilee, he went and begged Jesus to come to Capernaum to heal his son, who was about to die. Jesus asked, "Will you never believe in me unless you see miraculous signs and wonders?" The official pleaded, "Lord, please come now before my little boy dies." Then Jesus told him, "Go back home. Your son will

live!" And the man believed what Jesus said and started home. While the man was on his way, some of his servants met him with the news that his son was alive and well. He asked them when the boy had begun to get better, and they replied, "Yesterday afternoon at one o'clock his fever suddenly disappeared!" Then the father realized that that was the very time Jesus had told him, "Your son will live." And he and his entire household believed in Jesus.

John 4:46-53 NLT

The point to be made in this Scripture is that this man was not a true believer at first. He came to Jesus in desperation because his son was dying. Then, through the healing of his son, he and the rest of his entire household did become true believers in Jesus.

The miracles and gifts of God have two basic purposes. First they are evidence of God's love and compassion towards us. Second, the Lord desires them to be used to help build faith in us to believe God's message of Salvation, which is "Repent and believe on the Lord Jesus Christ."

Jesus explained to the evil religious leaders of His day that all the church attendance and religious rituals and signs and wonders in the world cannot save us. They only serve to point us toward the Way of Salvation. The Holy Spirit's ministry and gifts are designed to draw us toward believing in and being obedient to Christ. If we then choose to reject Christ's call to repent and refuse to believe what He has to say, there are no more excuses for those who reject the message of the Son of God and return to wickedness.

AND HE GAVE THEM POWER

I have used the NLT version of Mark 6 here for ease of reading, but where the NLT uses the word "authority", the King James Version uses the phrase "gave them power" in a battle sense. The Greek word used here refers to whacking and beating an opponent, so Jesus not only gave them authority over evil spirits, but a real spiritual ability to do battle with them in the spiritual realm and beat them into submission. If you think that this means that everyone who has the faith to minister in the power of

God is automatically saved, do not forget that the traitor Judas Iscariot was ministering in power right alongside the other eleven and look how he ended up.

> And he was amazed at their unbelief. Then Jesus went from village to village, teaching the people. And he called his twelve disciples together and began sending them out two by two, giving them authority to cast out evil spirits... So the disciples went out, telling everyone they met to repent of their sins and turn to God. And they cast out many demons and healed many sick people, anointing them with olive oil. Mark 6:6-13 NLT

In Chapter 9 of the Gospel of Luke there is a parallel account of Jesus sending out His twelve disciples and in this passage, the word "power" is translated from the Greek word "dunamis", meaning "miraculous mighty power. Fittingly, dunamis is the root origin of our modern words dynamic, dynamo and dynamite. This is the same word that Jesus uses when he explains to His disciples that even though He would be leaving us, Father God will send the Holy Spirit to help us and give us dynamic power:

> ...He commanded them, "Do not leave Jerusalem until the Father sends you the gift he promised, as I told you before. John baptized with water, but in just a few days you will be baptized with the Holy Spirit."...you will receive power when the Holy Spirit comes upon you. And you will be my witnesses, telling people about me everywhere—in Jerusalem, throughout Judea, in Samaria, and to the ends of the earth." Acts1:4-8 NLT

MIRACULOUS SIGNS ARE TO BUILD OUR FAITH AND HELP US BELIEVE

The truth is that by and large the human race is a faithless and unbelieving species. Jesus rebuked His own disciples for doubting the

Word of God and the testimony of those who declared that He was risen from the dead. Even amongst His own disciples, some simply would not believe Jesus had risen until He performed the miracle of teleporting, materializing right into their midst behind locked doors. Until they saw Jesus themselves, talked with Him and touched Him, many of His own disciples refused to believe the testimony of others declaring that Jesus had risen from the dead:

> On the evening of that first day of the week, when the disciples were together, with the doors locked for fear of the Jewish leaders, Jesus came and stood among them and said, "Peace be with you!" After he said this, he showed them his hands and side. The disciples were overjoyed when they saw the Lord. Again Jesus said, "Peace be with you! As the Father has sent me, I am sending you." And with that he breathed on them and said, "Receive the Holy Spirit… Now Thomas (also known as Didymus), one of the Twelve, was not with the disciples when Jesus came. So the other disciples told him, "We have seen the Lord!" But he said to them, "Unless I see the nail marks in his hands and put my finger where the nails were, and put my hand into his side, I will not believe." A week later his disciples were in the house again, and Thomas was with them. Though the doors were locked, Jesus came and stood among them and said, "Peace be with you!" Then he said to Thomas, "Put your finger here; see my hands. Reach out your hand and put it into my side. Stop doubting and believe." Thomas said to him, "My Lord and my God!" Then Jesus told him, "Because you have seen me, you have believed; blessed are those who have not seen and yet have believed."
> John 20:19-29 NIV

> …he rebuked them for their lack of faith and their stubborn refusal to believe those who had seen him after he had risen. He said to them, "Go into all the world and

preach the gospel to all creation. Whoever believes and is baptized will be saved, but whoever does not believe will be condemned...After the Lord Jesus had spoken to them, he was taken up into heaven and he sat at the right hand of God...Then the disciples went out and preached everywhere, and the Lord worked with them and confirmed his word by the signs that accompanied it.

Mark 16:14-20 NIV

SIGNS AND WONDERS ARE STILL
NEEDED IN THE WORLD TODAY

It is a sad thing when those who profess to be Christian leaders have so little compassion for their fellow man that they claim that the miraculous gifts of the Holy Spirit have passed away and they are no longer needed today.

Look around you! The precious gifts of God are needed just as much today as they were needed in the first century A.D. Such statements of denial are almost as heartless as trying to use the Scriptures to blame those who are sick and oppressed when they don't get well after being prayed for. To make themselves look good, some Christian leaders have been vain enough to place further despair and condemnation upon those oppressed of Satan by suggesting that the victims did not have enough faith to get healed. Those who think this way will often quote Matthew or Mark to support what they teach.

And he did not do many miracles there because of their lack of faith. Matthew 13:58 NIV

And he could there do no mighty work, save that he laid his hands upon a few sick folk, and healed them. And he marveled because of their unbelief...Mark 6:5-6 KJV

We see here that in Matthew it says that Jesus did not do many miracles and in Mark it says that He could not do any mighty work. In both cases it says that the reason was "because of their unbelief". The argument is then given by some people is that if Jesus Himself was not able to heal people when they do not have enough faith, how can **we** be successful?

This is what happens when people take Scriptures out of context and try to twist them to justify what they have chosen to believe regardless of whether or not it is what the Bible actually teaches. Sometimes our faith can influence God to move on our behalf, but Jesus Christ does not **need** our faith to perform miracles. Neither is He hindered from performing miracles if our faith is weak.

Even though Jesus remarked about the lack of faith in his own disciples, He still healed those who were brought to him. When the father of the demon-possessed child came to Jesus, admitting his own lack of faith and asking for help, Jesus healed and delivered the boy.

When the demon-possessed man came running out of the tombs, there was no faith involved on the part of the victim. There was only compassion on Christ's part to see that the man needed to be set free from the demons that were tormenting him. The same thing occurs at the pool of Bethesda. The crippled man did not come to Jesus in faith. Jesus came to him and healed him out of compassion, warning him to go and sin no more lest some worse thing should come upon him.

What about those whom Jesus raised from the dead? Dead people have no faith to respond to Jesus. They have no faith at all left to respond in this life. They are dead. Yet Jesus still had the power to raise them up. No, the true meaning of Matthew 13 and Mark 6 can only be obtained when we look at the portions of Scripture that have been deliberately left out by those who are in error.

THERE IS A DIFFERENCE BETWEEN WHAT GOD IS UNABLE TO DO AND WHAT GOD WILL NOT DO.

God is omnipotent. God is able do anything He wants to do. He does not require one iota of human faith to perform signs and wonders. Therefore, when these passages talk about Jesus not being able to perform many signs and wonders in His home town, we should be looking for another explanation other than Christ's own ability. The explanation we are looking for is included in the very same passages of Scripture.

In order to understand the true meaning of these passages, it is important to know the settings in which they occur. Jesus had been travelling for some time performing signs and wonders all throughout the land of Israel and then He returns to His home town where His own people then **reject Jesus as the Messiah**. They become offended at Jesus, rather than believing in Him. The key Scripture portion in both of these passages is that the people became "offended" in Jesus:

> And they were offended in him...
> Matthew 13:57 KJV
> ...And they were offended at him Mark 6:3 KJV

Hopefully, you are beginning to see that these Scriptures have nothing to do with Christ's actual ability to perform signs and wonders. They are talking about the fact that Jesus Christ will not override the free will of those who choose to reject Him. The kind of unbelief and the kind of offense being talked about here is the deliberate rejection of Jesus Himself as God's Redeemer.

Jesus **will not force Himself** upon anyone who refuses to believe in Him and His ministry. The reason that not many miracles were performed in Jesus' home town is that they did not want to believe in Him. They chose to personally reject Jesus as the Messiah. Therefore in that situation Jesus could not and would not override their rejection of Him because God is a God of love and freedom, not force and compulsion.

BELIEVING IN JESUS GIVES HIM PERMISSION TO ACT EVEN WHEN OUR FAITH IS LACKING.

Aside from the aforementioned experience with my trip to the U.S. and praying for my father-in-law, the only exposure that I had before 1981 regarding the signs and wonders of God was what I had seen on TV. There was really no way to verify how much (if any) of it was real and how much was a product of hype, hysteria and hucksterism.

For years I had listened to local preachers who taught that the time of signs and wonders and miracles and gifts of the Holy Spirit were over.

However, as more and more local ministers and TV preachers around the world are beginning to research the Scriptures and starting to disagree with those who refuse to believe the Word of God, things are beginning to change in corporate Christianity worldwide.

More and more signs and wonders are starting to manifest in the lives of those who choose to have faith in God's Word. God loves to respond to our faith. I have found that when we step out in even the smallest amount of faith to believe God's Word and act on it, God then steps up to confirm to us that His Word is true. I am telling you that signs and wonders are still happening today. I have seen it happen over and over again, and the Holy Spirit is a key participant in the miracles of God.

I knew from my personal history that I had virtually no power in my own life to overcome my addictions and resist my own urges to sin. I knew that I needed something from God to help me overcome my own wicked nature if the rest of my life was going to be different from the ways that had brought me to desolation and suicidal thoughts during my former life.

I realized I needed the power of the Holy Spirit in my life if I was going to overcome sin. I told God that I wanted it all, everything that God has available for me to use, including speaking in tongues if that was what God wanted to give me. I was through doubting God and holding back through unbelief. I invited the Holy Spirit into my life, not just to be there, but to give me power over the areas where I had tried and failed to serve God for many years.

Then gradually, as I learned to trust God and trust the Holy Spirit's guidance, things started to happen in my life and in the lives of those around me. God began to prove to me that He is the same yesterday, today and forever. Today I know for sure that He still performs miracles. I have seen it happen over and over again.

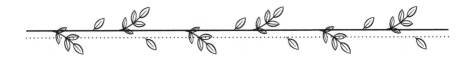

CHAPTER 19

A God of Miracles

BELIEVING GOD'S WORD ABOUT SIGNS AND WONDERS OPENS THE DOOR FOR MIRACLES AND WONDERS TO OCCUR

Before 1981 I had almost no experience in seeing God moving in signs and wonders because I had previously only been in contact with people who did not really believe that God still moves in this way in modern society. That all changed when I decided to believe God and chose to begin fellowshipping with those who also believed God.

I have been a Christian leader now for over thirty years and I still do not see supernatural signs and wonders every day in my life. Yet that does not mean that I have never seen God do the miraculous. Over the years I have seen God move sovereignly in many different ways, so I felt that it would be an encouragement to the reader for me to include some of those testimonies in this chapter. Hopefully it will help build your faith to believe that God is still a God of the miraculous and we never know when He will prove it to us.

FAITH COMES BY HEARING

One thing that I have learned over the years is that there is a correlation between how much we see regarding God's power and God's gifts and who we decide to associate with. When I spent little time with God, doubted God myself and surrounded myself with people who doubted God there were no signs and wonders.

Then when I chose to start praying more, believing God, obeying God and associating with people who still believe that God still works in wondrous ways, I began to experience the power of God in my life on many occasions. One of the reasons that God encourages us to not forsake gathering together with other people is that being around other people of faith and hearing their testimonies helps to increase our own faith in God and what God can do. Then we begin to see the miraculous happen. God loves to respond to faith.

GOD, DELIVER ME
FROM ADDICTION!

That was my prayer to God on that night when I turned my life over to Jesus in 1981. I had tried unsuccessfully over and over for years to be set free from my addictions, but all that time I had not really been trusting God.

That night God made a promise to me that if I repented, if I made a choice to start believing God and obeying God, Jesus would set me free from the chains that Satan had bound me with ever since I was introduced to the lure of pornography, alcohol and drugs as a young child.

God promised that He would help me overcome these things and the evil spirits behind them. Jesus would give me victory over all the power of Satan and his temptations as long as I was willing to continue to listen to the Word of God and walk in obedience. That night I made a decision that I wasn't going to be bound by Satan's power any more. When Satan tried to re-assert his addictions in my life, I refused to yield. When the pressure to sin seemed unbearable, I made the decision that "even if it kills me" I was going to serve God.

Over the years God has remained faithful to His promise. Today I am free from every addiction that once ruled my life. Furthermore, I have seen God do the same thing over and over again for many different people and it doesn't matter what kind of addiction it is. If we are totally committed to repent, to believe and obey the Lord, God always keeps His end of the bargain.

My own mother was a good example. After seeing God turn my life around, Mom accepted Jesus and received the Holy Spirit when she was in her sixties and God mercifully delivered her from a lifelong struggle with depression and addictions to cigarettes and alcohol. She lived the remainder of her life as a sober, joyful, solid, dedicated Christian.

I have also come in contact with many people over the years who testify of God delivering them from addictions of all kinds, prescription and hard drug addictions, sexual addictions, self-harm addictions, violent addictions, even TV and video game addictions. In every case God has proven that His Word is still true, yesterday, today and forever. You might not classify deliverance from addictions as a miracle, but I do. Deep in my heart I know that if God had not intervened, I would still be a prisoner of my sin and headed for hell today.

Are you a person who has managed to escape addiction on your own? Good for you, but even that will not save you. God has something even more valuable for us than being addiction-free. Of what true value is it to get free of our addictions for the remaining few years of our mortal lives only to spend eternity separated from God? God's Word tells us that the world is already condemned, but if we repent of our sins and accept Jesus Christ as our Savior. Heaven is our reward and the Earth is our inheritance. Why not add salvation to your victory over your addictions?

If you still need to hear of miracles happening in order to believe that salvation through Jesus Christ is real and God still performs wonders today, here are just a few that I have experienced in my own life. I hope that my testimony to you about them will help to build your faith to believe that God does love us and wants us to know that if we pray to Him in faith, He still wants to move in signs and wonders today.

GOD ONCE PERFORMED A MIRACLE
OF TELEPORTATION IN MY LIFE

There are several recorded instances of God performing miracles of teleportation in the Bible. In John 6 we see the disciples in the midst of a lake when a terrible storm arises and their boat is in danger of sinking, so Jesus comes to them walking on the water and the moment that He steps into the boat, the whole boat is immediately transported or "teleported" to safety on the other shore of the lake.

Then there is the record after Christ's resurrection when the disciples are all meeting behind locked doors for fear of the Jews and Jesus teleports Himself inside the locked room. Lastly we have the Scriptural testimony of the time that the Apostle Philip was ministering to the Ethiopian eunuch in the middle of the desert. After the man accepts Christ, Philip suddenly vanishes and finds himself in the next town. I guess that God just decided to bless Philip by sparing him the long hike through the desert to his next destination.

As fascinating as I found these stories to be, I had never imagined that anything like that would ever happen to me, and yet it did. I was in my little Datsun pickup on my way home from the next town. It was a dark night and I had just started into a notoriously sharp S curve known as Hagman's corner, named after the farmer who owned the surrounding land. Then I saw something that scared the wits out of me. There framed in my headlights were three full grown cows.

There was one cow on my side of the road, one straddling the middle line and one in the opposing lane. There was no time to stop, no way to get between them, and driving off the shoulder was out of the question because there was a deep gulley down to a creek on both sides. It would have meant a horrendous crash and possible death if I had tried to take that route of escape.

There was no way out of the situation so I gripped the steering wheel as hard as I could and closed my eyes tightly to protect them from flying glass. Then I braced myself for the massive impact that was going to occur from hitting a thousand pound cow at sixty miles an hour. At the same time, I shouted one word at the top of my lungs "JESUS".

It only took a second or two to realize that something miraculous had happened because there was no impact. I thought that maybe God had moved one of the cows out of the way so I looked in the rear view mirror and saw that they were all still completely blocking the road. It was then that I realized that God had not moved the cows, He had teleported me, truck and all from one side of the cows to the other side of the cows. Thank you Jesus. I have never again experienced anything quite like it since that day, but I am grateful that God heard my prayer on that particular day.

GOD KNOWS HOW TO FIND THINGS

There are three instances that particularly stand out in my memory where God directed me to find something. The first was when we were conducting an open air church service and concert in the ballfield of a small town north of where I live. One of the ladies in the worship team was upset that she had lost her glasses somewhere that day and she had no idea when or where she lost them. As she could hardly see a thing without them, I encouraged the group that we should all pray for the Lord's help to find the glasses.

Immediately after prayer I felt led of the Lord to walk all the way through the outfield and into the knee high grass that surrounded the ballpark. At a certain point, I stopped and looked down, and you guessed it, there were the glasses. We had no idea how they got there. There was no way that we would have ever found those glasses on our own. I know that it was God who helped me.

On another occasion we were upstairs praying in our church when some brazen thief walked into the main sanctuary downstairs and stole the guitar and amplifier of the president of the Bible College who was scheduled to be ministering on the praise and worship team that day. Of course, the first thing that we did was to pray for the Lord to help us get the guitar back.

Now let me paint the picture for you. I live in a city with a population of over a hundred thousand people. There are over a dozen pawn shops in the city, but after prayer I told the group that I believed that the Lord was leading me to go to one particular pawn shop, so they said go. I got in my truck, drove to the shop, found the very distinctive guitar and amp sitting there and paid the pawn shop owner the $20 that it had cost him for the items. Then I brought them back with me to return them again to a very happy owner.

GOD KNOWS HOW TO FIND PEOPLE

The third situation involved finding a particular person during a missionary trip to Guatemala. Before I left Canada, one of my pastors told me of a certain missionary who was doing a good work down in Guatemala. They asked me to try to contact him while I was down there to see if there was some way that we could help him. I was then given a sum of money to distribute wherever I felt the Holy Spirit was leading me to donate while I was in Guatemala.

There were a lot of answers to prayer surrounding that trip to Guatemala, but this one example shows how God can not only find people, He has great timing as well. After arriving in Guatemala, I actually managed to reach the man's home by phone but the person answering the phone did not speak English. I only knew enough Spanish to glean from the conversation that it was the housekeeper speaking. The man was ministering somewhere up in the mountains and they would not be able to reach him until he returned.

I was still convinced that the Lord wanted me to meet with this man so I made the 200 km bus ride from Guatemala City to the man's home city of Quetzaltenango, trusting in faith that the Lord would make a way for me to find the man. Upon arriving in Quetzaltenango, I went to the Canadian Consulate and found out that they did know of the man, but did not know where his office was or how to contact him. I was out of ideas, so I turned to prayer.

Many Central American cities have large town squares with monuments and a park area in the center, so I left the consulate and started walking around the perimeter of the town square. I fervently prayed to God, letting God know that if He wanted me to get in contact with this man, I was out of options and God was going to have to make it happen.

I continued praying as I walked around the square and was almost back to where I started when I looked down a side street and saw a sign identifying a Spanish/English school so I went inside. If nothing else (I thought) at least someone there will speak English and maybe they would be able to help me.

"Oh yes", they said. "We know him. His office is right across the street" and the man pointed to a building on the other side of the street with a tiny sign on the door. As he was saying this, a pickup truck pulled up to the door and someone went inside. I thanked the man at the school and rushed over to talk to whoever was there.

This was the man I had been looking for. He had only driven back down to the office to get something that he needed and was immediately headed back out miles into the mountains. Ten minutes earlier or ten minutes later and I would have missed him. This was no coincidence. If I had not walked around the town square praying and if I had not gone into the school at the exact time that I did, this man would have come and gone and I would have never found him, but God knows how to arrange divine appointments.

I accepted the missionary's invitation to accompany him back up into the mountains to see the work that they were doing there. He explained to me that they had felt the Lord's leading to raise up a building in a rural village that would serve a multi- purpose as a community hall, source of clean water and place of worship.

It would be a gathering place where people could come for clean safe water to use for drinking and there was an outdoor laundry area with concrete tables and sinks where people could wash their clothes. Inside they would be able to hold village meetings and church services.

His ministry had proceeded with the project on faith, trusting that God would provide for the needs as they arose. The well and pump were installed and the water was flowing. The lumber for the walls and the material for the roof were all purchased and sitting there ready to be installed, but that is as far as they had been able to go. There were no more immediate funds to purchase all of the concrete that would be necessary to complete the floor of the building and the base for the washing and drinking areas.

When I asked him how much that this would cost and then informed him that the Lord had provided me with the funds to help them complete the building, they were most grateful. That evening, dozens of villagers came from miles around to participate in a beautiful worship service on the building site. Then the next day I said my goodbyes and headed back to Guatemala City to see what other adventures the Lord would have for me next. God is good. I'll tell you a little more about Guatemala later on in the book.

GOD STILL HEALS TODAY

I can't tell you why God does not heal everyone who comes for prayer. I can't even tell you why I don't get healed every time I ask for prayer, but I can tell you that God has healed me at various times during my life and I have also seen and heard testimony of God healing numerous others, even in the small church of less than fifty people that I attended back in the early 1980's.

One of the ladies there told of how the doctors had diagnosed her with a tipped womb and informed her that the child she was soon about to bear would definitely have to be delivered by caesarian section, so the whole church prayed that God would heal this condition and after about four hours labor, out popped a healthy baby, no caesarian necessary.

Another pregnant lady managed to get herself crushed between their truck and a cement wall because the truck had been left running and her toddler had slipped it into gear as she was walking by. This time the doctors told her that her several internal injuries and injuries to the baby were severe and the baby could be born abnormal or even die during childbirth. Again the church prayed, and again a perfectly healthy baby boy was born when the time was right.

There was also the time when I went to pick my mother up for church and found her half-dressed and crying because she wanted to go to church but her arthritis had become so bad that she was not able to zip up her dress anymore. I helped her finish dressing and encouraged her to go forward to have her arthritis prayed for.

It was a wonderful service and when Pastor Claudia invited people to come forward for prayer after the service, Mom went up to the front. Then the pastor and entire church gathered around Mom and started praying for her. Suddenly Mom collapsed and hit the floor so hard that I was concerned that she might have hurt herself, but no, that was not the case.

Mom came back up bouncing and jumping around and praising God like an eight year old and she never again suffered from arthritis for the rest of her life. Right up to the time of her death, she remained flexible enough to put one hand behind her head and one behind her back and touch fingers. I certainly can't do that, and I am sure that most of you can't either. In her early years mom had taught dancing until the pain began to restrict her movement. In her later years, she danced pain free before the Lord as she worshipped Him.

GOD TURNED A PERSONAL TRAGEDY
INTO A TESTIMONY OF HEALING

A couple of things that I have learned about God over the years is that God does not always do things the same way. In fact I believe that Jesus deliberately healed people in many different ways to demonstrate to us that there is no particular formula or technique that can be used to make healing happen. Our job is simply to ask for God's help and not give up, even if the answer doesn't come right away, or come in the way we expected it to.

Let me give you a couple of examples from my own life. About three years after I got saved, through a moment of ignorance and carelessness I received second degree burns to my hands and right leg and third degree burns to my left calf and the back of my knee.

As a matter of fact, when the accident happened there was no water around to put out the fire out. If it had not been for the selfless act of an unsaved friend falling on the flames with his own body and smothering them, there was a very real possibility that I could have died that day or been severely crippled for the rest of my life.

As it was, I ended up in hospital with second and third degree burns. I had to endure the agony of having the dead skin removed and weeks of rehab in the hospital before they sent me home unable to use that leg at all. After keeping an eye on it for a while, my doctor informed me one Monday morning that the leg was not healing.

Without skin grafts, he said that it did not look like I was going to regain use of the leg and I could even lose the leg to gangrene. Now, I don't know how much you know about skin grafts, but in those days they used to cut a piece off your backside and use it to try to grow new skin on your leg, not at all a pleasant experience to look forward to.

I didn't want to be crippled for the rest of my life, but I did not like the idea of going through the skin graft process either so I called Pastor Claudia and asked if she and the rest of the prayer team would please pray for God to heal my leg. She said they would do that and I thought that this would be the end of it. Then about a half hour later there was a knock on the door. When Mom answered the door, in came about a half dozen ladies and an accordion. They had all driven twenty miles together to come and anoint me with oil and pray for me in person.

First of all we had an impromptu praise and worship session that was quite beautiful. Then they anointed me with oil, laid hands on me and began praying. I felt the power of God begin to flow through my body. I'm telling you that these women were real prayer warriors. They knew how to pray. By the time they had left the house, I was sure that God had touched me.

The next day I had another appointment with my doctor. I went in with high spirits but my hopes were crushed when he told me that there was no change and he was going to book me into the hospital the next day for the skin grafts to make sure that I did not get gangrene or permanently lose the use of my leg. What a letdown that was, but I resigned myself to what seemed to be the medical facts.

The day after that, I hobbled to my car on crutches and drove the fifty miles to the closest burn center where they put me on a gurney, stuck an I.V. needle into my arm and wheeled me into the operating room. Then the doctor unwrapped the bandages from my leg to prepare it for surgery. As soon as the doctor saw my leg, he remarked that he didn't really understand it, but the leg was now healing well and they would not have to perform the skin graft. They pulled the I.V., out of my arm, rewrapped my leg and sent me home. I was on the road to recovery. Thank you Jesus.

DON'T GIVE UP!
SOMETIMES GOD HEALS IN STAGES

It's true. My burned leg was an excellent example of God healing in stages. Hebrews 11:1 tells us that faith is the substance of things hoped for and the evidence of things unseen. God wants us to continue to have faith in Him even when we don't see any immediate results. The interesting thing is that in this case God performed my healing in two stages. The first stage was when the doctors sent me home because my leg was starting to heal and I would not need skin grafts.

After I got home, my own doctor informed me that even though my leg was starting to heal, it was still going to be a long and painful rehab that would require daily application of ointment and keeping the leg completely wrapped in burn dressings and bandages for a period of up to a year or two before the healing process would be complete.

I did unsuccessfully try a few times to exercise faith that God would immediately complete the healing process. Each time I tried removing the bandages for any extended time, the skin on my leg would dry up and crack and bleed until I had to give in and re-apply the ointment and bandages again. I was grateful to God for sparing me the skin grafts, but in the back of my mind I was thinking that God was now putting me through this long and painful rehab because of the sinful life that I had once led.

I blamed my past sins as the reason for God not completely healing me now. I had gone from being a sinner to having a bit of a martyr complex. I decided that I was ready to suffer for another two years if that is what God wanted of me, but God had something else in mind, something much better.

The accident actually happened about two months before I started Bible College. I now firmly believe that it was an attack of Satan designed to keep me out of the ministry, but it didn't work. I was still on crutches when the first semester of Bible College started, but I made it there.

Then a short time into my first year at Bible School, the Lord arranged another divine appointment. It was an experience that would teach me a little humility through someone that I needed to listen to if I wanted to be healed completely.

Not long after I started Bible College we were told that we would be having a guest speaker that week and the name sounded familiar to me. Once the person showed up, I recognized him as the man who had wired the trailer that I was living in with such incompetence that you had to go right outside on the front porch to turn the living room light off when you went to bed at night, really annoying when it was raining or cold and snowing outside. I was not impressed.

GOD TEACHES ME A LESSON ABOUT
HUMILITY AND JUDGING OTHERS

My first reaction was "What could this person possibly have to say that would be of any value to me?" Immediately, the Lord stopped me in my tracks, reminding me that I had made many mistakes in my life and He was still using me. God told me that this man was a chosen vessel and what he had to say was important for me to learn. "Listen to him."

It turned out that the bulk of the man's message was explaining that God's love toward us and His desire to heal and deliver us is unconditional. God's desire for us to be whole has no bearing whatsoever on our past sins. It was like God was using this man as a guiding light for me to help me change my thinking. I began to realize that God did not want me to suffer for another two years. God really wanted to heal me completely. It was like a switch was turned on in my faith and I suddenly realized that I was being healed right then.

I went home that night and thanked God for His healing touch. Then I took the bandages off and fell into a deep sleep. When I woke up in the morning my skin was soft, healed and I have never had trouble with my leg since that time. I still have the visible scars from the accident, but the skin is soft and my leg still works fine thirty-five years later.

God taught me something useful that day about vanity and judging others. When the preacher asked the next day if anyone wanted prayer for healing, the Lord put it in my heart to testify before everybody of what God had done for me as a result of this man's message and encouraged others to believe as well. Then I went up for prayer with everyone else to demonstrate to God that I was willing to listen to Him regardless of the vessel He chose to use to speak to me.

The truth be known, God will even speak to us through unsaved people at times. If we are wise, we will learn to set our pride aside, humble ourselves and listen to the Word of God regardless of the source, even if it is a new believer, an unbeliever, or some drunk or drug addict lying in a gutter. The wise will listen for God's Word, whatever the source. I am not suggesting that you believe everything that every person, Christian or preacher says. The best course of action is to be open to listen, compare what they say with what God has to say in His Word and then eat the meat and spit out the bones.

IF YOUR CAUSE IS GOOD, NEVER GIVE UP PRAYING. GOD IS LISTENING.

It doesn't matter if you are praying for guidance, finances, healing or salvation of friends and relatives, don't stop. Don't give up. I have seen God heal people instantly. I have seen God heal people in stages, and in one case in my life I had to keep praying for twelve years before anything happened. There are numerous cases in the Bible where people prayed and trusted God for years, and one day God moves.

In spite of all the other blessings that I had enjoyed from God since 1981, there was one area of my body that the Devil did not want to let go of. It was the bottoms of my feet. In the early 1970's I had come in contact with a plantar virus. As a result of this, over the years I had developed plantar warts on my heels that had grown to the size of silver dollars and were very deep. I don't know how much you know about plantar warts, but these giant warts on my heels were a real problem. When they get that big and run that deep they hurt you when you walk.

Over the years I tried every medical treatment available. First they tried to remove them surgically. They came back bigger. Then they tried to use liquid nitrogen to kill them by freezing. My feet hurt so badly after the surgery and the liquid nitrogen that the cures were worse than having the warts and yet still they came back bigger than ever.

The last thing that the doctors tried was ultrasound. It wasn't that painful but it did not work either. Then the doctors gave me the news that with some people, nothing works. They warned me that the warts could keep getting bigger and more painful until eventually I might not be able to walk any more.

Well, maybe the doctors couldn't cure this, but I knew someone who could. I kept praying for 12 years for God to heal me. I put my embarrassment aside and kept asking other believers to pray that God would get rid of the warts. Then one morning it happened. I woke up and my feet felt different, the painful discomfort was gone and when I looked at my feet, all of the warts were completely gone. The night before they had been as big and bad as ever and the next morning they were gone and they have never come back again. Thank you Jesus. Never give up praying if your cause is just. God hears you.

CHAPTER 20

Preparing For Ministry

GOD KNOWS HOW TO GUIDE OUR FINANCES

When I repented and turned to God in 1981, it was a hundred percent commitment. I did not know how or when or where, but I knew that I wanted to serve God from that time forth. I was sure that God wanted me to attend Bible College, but before I could do that, I believed that the Lord wanted me to pay off my debts and I owed over $15,000.

I had never even managed to save a thousand dollars at once in my life, so I asked for the Lord's help and wisdom to make it happen. I knew I couldn't do it by myself and to this day I really don't know how it all came together, but somehow it did.

By 1985 the Lord had enabled me to pay off the fifteen thousand dollars that I owed plus an additional fifteen thousand that was my ex-wife's portion of our debt. Not only was everything completely paid off, I had eighteen thousand dollars in cash left over to pay for the expenses of going to Bible College. That's the most money that I had ever had at once in my entire life.

Now, raising $48,000 in three years might not seem like much by today's standards, but remember, this was back in the day when you could buy a house in our neighborhood for less money than this, and the minimum wage in Canada was under five dollars an hour. I have no doubts whatsoever that God worked things out to enable this to happen.

GOD KNOWS HOW TO DIRECT OUR PATHS AND OPEN DOORS FOR US

The next big step for me after I got saved was to find a Bible College, not just any Bible College, but the one God wanted me to go to. This was not a decision that I took lightly. I did some serious research on this, checking out colleges in Kelowna, Vancouver, Alberta and even one in San Jose California. They were all good, but for some reason I believed that the Lord wanted me in Kelowna, BC.

This was somewhat baffling to me because the Bible College in Kelowna was fundamentalist in their teachings and I was definitely charismatic in my beliefs. Yet when I informed them of my belief that the gifts of the Holy Spirit were still relevant today, they accepted my application anyway. Okay then. Everything seemed set. I supposed that this was where God wanted me. Theologically there were colleges in other cities that would have been a better fit for me, but somehow I felt that God wanted me in Kelowna.

Even though Kelowna had close to a zero vacancy rate, Mom had decided that she wanted to move to Kelowna with me so I said "Let's go!" Somehow God worked it out that we were able to find an affordable house for my mother and I to live in. With the Lord's help, the money I had saved was adequate for a down payment and there would be enough left over for expenses while I attended my first year at Bible College.

The next step was to find a church to attend. Even though I had been accepted at a fundamentalist college, I was certain that the Lord wanted me to attend a church that believed in the Baptism and gifts of the Holy Spirit. I had heard of such a church in Kelowna that sounded like what I was looking for, so I went in to speak with them.

The secretary directed me to three gentlemen who were talking together in a side area of the office, one of whom was the senior pastor of the church. I explained to him that I believed God was directing me to attend Bible College in Kelowna and I was looking for a charismatic church to attend. I told him the important details of my checkered past, holding nothing back. Then I explained to him that I now wanted to serve God for the rest of my life. I noticed that all three men were smiling. In fact they seemed rather amused by what I was saying and I was about to find out why.

The pastor told me that I would be welcome to attend his church. Then he introduced me to the other two men, the president and vice-president of a brand new charismatic Bible College in Kelowna. It was so new that they had just had their first graduating class and had not even advertised yet. That's why I did not know about them. Right then and there I knew that this was where God wanted me to be. I was still on crutches, but I was headed for Bible College, the one that God wanted me to attend.

IN THIS WORLD YOU WILL
HAVE TRIBULATION

I get annoyed when I hear preachers telling people that all you have to do is believe in Jesus and you'll be healthy, wealthy and wise for the rest of your life. To hear them talk, serving Jesus will be all wine, roses, lollipops and rainbows as long as you tithe to their church and give generous offerings to their ministry on top of that. No wonder people get so disillusioned with Christianity. Jesus didn't promise this. In John 16:33 He tells us that in this world you are going to have tribulation. You will make mistakes that will cause you problems. Bad things will happen during your life that are not your fault. You will run across people (even other professing Christians) who will mistreat you and dislike you without cause. You can still get sick or become physically injured. Becoming a Christian doesn't change any of that.

We still live in a world troubled by evil. The Lord has not promised us that our life as a Christian will always be fair and painless. God has healed me of many things over the years, but I still get hurt and sick on occasion and have to suffer through it. I cracked a rib the other day, and as I am writing this I know that unless God performs a miracle I am in for about three or four weeks of pain and discomfort before it gets better. Sometimes life is like that. I also know that unless Jesus arrives soon, there will come a day in my future when I will be old enough that I will get sick and I will not get better. I will die. I am OK with that because I know that the real promise of Christianity is not that this mortal life will be perfect after we accept Jesus.

The true promise of Christianity is that when we accept Jesus Christ, He will give us the Holy Spirit to help us deal with any and every obstacle that comes our way in this life. Then, after our resurrection Jesus has eternal blessings for us that will never end. This corrupted body will be instantly changed from corruptible to incorruptible, transformed from mortal to immortal, and Jesus has all of eternity to more than compensate every single believer on Earth for every single bit of suffering that we endure during our few decades of life in these bodies. Jesus has promised us an eternity of joy unspeakable and full of glory to make up for the worst things that could ever happen to us on this side of heaven, and God keeps His promises.

SOMETIMES THINGS DON"T GO ACCORDING TO PLAN

When I first came to Kelowna, I had everything planned out. I would put the down payment on the house. Mom and I would share the cost of the mortgage payment and I would be able to use the remaining eight thousand dollars in my savings account to take care of my share of the mortgage payments and my expenses for the first year of Bible College.

Then the bank pulled a fast one on me. They told me that because I was not working, they would not OK the mortgage unless I allowed them to put a lien on my savings account. I was not going to be able to touch that money in the bank, even though it was mine.

I'm telling you, this really burned my bacon. It was my money yet I couldn't touch it and it was only a few months until my first semester at Bible College started. Now I had to find a job in Kelowna, a place with a high unemployment rate. To make a long story short, I did find a full time job working for a Christian businessman until it was time for my semester to start.

Furthermore, it turned out that the man liked me so much that when I started Bible College he handed me the key to the factory. He told me that I could come in any hours I chose and work part time while I was attending

College. This ended up being very beneficial to me during the two years I was taking classes. Often, something that starts out as a hardship can turn out to be a great blessing in the end.

Another example of this came when I wanted to refinance the house mortgage. Interest rates were terrible in those days. I was paying thirteen and a half percent interest on the mortgage. Then the interest rates dropped the next year to eleven percent but the bank refused to refinance at the lower rate and still refused to release the lien on my savings account even though I had dealt with that name-brand of bank for decades, ever since I was sixteen years old.

I presented my predicament as a prayer request at school and another Bible school student gladly loaned me the funds needed for my second year of tuition. Then I found another bank that I had never dealt with before. They took over the mortgage at the lower interest rate without requiring any guarantee, so I got my eight thousand dollars back to repay the other student and help with my costs for the second year. Things might not go the way that we originally planned it, but in the end, God works all things together for good.

BIBLE COLLEGE, GOD'S CHRISTIAN IMMERSION SCHOOL

I really loved the first year of Bible School. This was a school that was born of the Spirit of God only two years before I started attending and was a powerful influence in the city of Kelowna and throughout Western Canada. Five days a week most of us would all meet for prayer and worship in the mornings and then go to class for teaching on many aspects of Christian life and ministry.

Many of the teachers were highly anointed men and women of God, as were the guest speakers who would come in to teach a class once or twice a week. The guest speakers were usually evangelists or missionaries who were back home between trips, but sometimes they were just mature Christians from the community who were welcomed to give their input.

It was a school with a real vision for the Lord. At least that's the way it was in the beginning. There was a huge diversity of students as well. They were everything from zealous brand new converts, to ministry candidates, to long-time believers who were interested in expanding their knowledge and walk with God.

In addition to classes there was also the opportunity (for those who were interested) to minister in music, witnessing, teaching and evangelism over the weekends locally and at numerous other cities across the province. I have a decent baritone voice and good vocal range so I volunteered to minister in music and was soon invited to be one of the lead singers of the music ministry.

One of the best things about Bible College was that it kept me immersed in the things of God during my formative Christian years and gave me the good foundation of Christian doctrine and theology that I now teach to other people. It was in Bible College where I learned that the dominant gifts of the Holy Spirit in my life are teaching, prophecy and discerning of spirits. These are gifts that would turn out to be both a blessing and a challenge for me as school and life went on.

THERE ARE SPIRITUAL CONFLICTS
EVEN IN BIBLE COLLEGE

The Bible College was the dream of a godly man who had little credentials and qualifications in the natural but a strong vision from God to raise up a charismatic Bible College in Kelowna and God blessed his efforts. The school was initially a vibrant, alive and powerful move of the Holy Spirit and students were drawn to it from all over Canada. There were even a few from other countries.

During the first couple of years, quite a number of these students went on to enter the ministry in many different places and the school was growing rapidly, as much by word of mouth reputation as by any other means. In fact, the church that I now attend as an associate pastor over 30 years later was planted by one of the Bible College students from the first graduating class. Yet the College itself was not without its problems.

Unfortunately, over time the spirit of vanity managed to get a foothold in the College. There were a few bad apples in the bunch, leaders who had the education and the credentials, but who did not understand or want the Holy Spirit's presence and ministry in the school.

They managed to convince the president of the Bible College that it would be better for the reputation and growth of the College if greater emphasis was placed on respectability, learning and knowledge and less on the active ministry in the gifts and moving of the Holy Spirit.

By the time I arrived in 1985, these people were already actively trying to undermine the Holy Spirit and working to create a rift between the College and the local charismatic assembly that had originally sponsored the work and provided the facilities for the College to use.

THINGS STARTED IN THE SPIRIT
CANNOT BE FINISHED IN THE FLESH

One thing about the ministry of the Holy Spirit moving in signs and wonders is that it seriously disturbs the status quo. When the Holy Spirit begins to move in a gathering of people, there is an unseen spiritual conflict going on in the background. Things can get noisy, emotional and messy, but don't confuse a spiritual battle with disorder. When people get delivered from demons, it's disturbing when these things manifest until they are cast out. When people are healed of ailments that they have been suffering from for years, it's OK for a spiritual uproar of emotion and praise and prayer to pour out for a while.

We erupt in joyous pandemonium at sports events when someone puts a puck or a ball in a net or scores some points and we don't even think twice about it. Some people shed tears of joy when their team wins and tears of sorrow when they lose. If we can get that excited over our child on sports day or some millionaire putting a ball or puck into a goal, how much more excited should we be when someone who has been in bondage to Satan for years is set free by the power of God.

During my first year at Bible College, the Holy Spirit was still moving mightily through several teachers and students. His gifts were flowing in ministry to the help of numerous students and even some of the leaders. As mentioned before, I myself was physically healed, as were other people. Some were even delivered from demonic torment.

There were also words of wisdom, knowledge and prophecy given under the authority of the College leaders, but by far the most controversial situation was that occasionally during a praise and worship session, ministry time or prayer time, a demon would become exposed and manifest itself. Yes, it can happen, even in church or Bible College. I have close friends who were delivered from demon oppression while they were at Bible College. The only reason that it does not happen more often is that in many churches and seminaries nobody ever says anything that bothers the demons.

The solution to a demonic incident was for the students and teachers who understood what was happening to gather around the person who was afflicted and pray over them until the rotten thing was cast out and the person was set free spiritually.

Of course, this is a ministry that Satan is particularly opposed to because he wants to keep his victims under his control. He does not want people to be set free. Whenever demonic manifestation happened it had a tendency to upset some of the other students and teachers who didn't understand what was going on, didn't believe it was happening, or didn't want it happening in the school.

I am sure that there was a certain amount of fear involved at times, but there was more to it than that. I believe that some were vainly more concerned about presenting an image of respectability to the world than they were genuinely concerned with seeing people actually healed and delivered from the Devil.

Others had trouble believing that professing Christians could have a problem with demons, but Jesus warned that past, present and future sinful behavior opens the door for such things to happen regardless of what we claim to believe in. Jesus also testified that sometimes there is no particular sin involved in matters of demon oppression. Sometimes, Satan just chooses to target someone, yet God reminds us in His Word that Jesus is more powerful than the Devil.

Regardless of the original cause of the demonic oppression, the Bible makes it clear that God wants to show us His power, love and glory by delivering all who come to Him who are oppressed by the Devil. You can describe the problem however you want to label it, but the truth is that some people have a demonic influence in their life that is so strong that they need God's help to be set free of it.

DO NOT GRIEVE OR QUENCH
THE HOLY SPIRIT

In the Word of God we are warned not to grieve or quench the Holy Spirit. We grieve the Holy Spirit by sinning. We quench the Holy Spirit by not listening to Him and trying to shut Him up and shut Him down. This opposition to the Holy Spirit is a recipe for disaster, regardless of whether it involves a single person, a church, or an entire Bible College.

> Therefore each of you must put off falsehood and speak truthfully to your neighbor, for we are all members of one body. "In your anger do not sin": Do not let the sun go down while you are still angry, and do not give the devil a foothold. Anyone who has been stealing must steal no longer, but must work, doing something useful with their own hands, that they may have something to share with those in need. Do not let any unwholesome talk come out of your mouths, but only what is helpful for building others up according to their needs, that it may benefit those who listen. And do not grieve the Holy Spirit of God, with whom you were sealed for the day of redemption. Get rid of all bitterness, rage and anger, brawling and slander, along with every form of malice. Ephesians 4:25-31 NIV
>
> Do not quench the Spirit. Do not treat prophecies with contempt 1 Thessalonians 5:19-20 NIV

During my second year at the Bible College, numerous students (including myself) were discouraged from moving in their spiritual gifts as the Holy Spirit leads. As the emphasis was directed away from reliance upon the Holy Spirit and more toward scholasticism only, you could feel the original spiritual life of the place shriveling up and dying.

The rift continued to grow between the College and the local charismatic church that had been supporting the school from the beginning and there was talk of moving the College into its own facility in order to expand and distance the College from the people that had initially been such a help. It was a disturbing direction, but I decided to stick it out with the College until graduation. Then things got rough.

WE MUST OBEY GOD
RATHER THAN MEN

In Chapter 5 of the book of Acts the Word of God tells us of a time when the Spiritual leaders of Israel confront Peter and the rest of the Apostles to remind them that they had been warned not to preach and teach in the name of Jesus. This was their response:

> Then they brought the apostles before the high council, where the high priest confronted them. "We gave you strict orders never again to teach in this man's name!" he said. "Instead, you have filled all Jerusalem with your teaching about him, and you want to make us responsible for his death!" But Peter and the apostles replied, "We must obey God rather than any human authority. Acts 5:27-29 NLT

In the Scriptures we are encouraged to submit ourselves to those who are in authority over us but there will also come times during our lives when we will come to a crossroads and have to decide whether or not we are going to obey God or men.

It was less than two months before graduation. I had submitted to the authority of the leadership of the College and ceased moving in the gifts of the Holy Spirit as they had instructed me to do, praying all the time that God would raise up others to move in the Spirit, but that did not happen. The spiritual life had gone out of the place.

There had been no manifestation at all of the gifts of God in our midst for months. Then one day a charismatic healing evangelist was invited back to speak during the last class of the day. As the minister began testifying of all the wonderful things that God was doing overseas and how God was healing people and delivering many people of evil spirits, I started to feel spiritual life come back into the place, into my own bones and into those around me.

There was a spiritual electricity in the air that we had not experienced in a long, long time. Then at the end of the message, the evangelist began to pray and others joined in enthusiastically until there was a long silence and I clearly heard the voice of God saying "Prophesy!"

That started me arguing with God reminding Him that there were only two months left until graduation and I could get expelled for doing this, but still the silence persisted and God again said "Prophesy!" This time I opened my mouth.

I don't even remember what I said, but I do remember that immediately one of the new students fell on his knees before God and confessed that he was involved in sinful practices that were not of God and he begged to be prayed for so that he could be set free. This set off a chain reaction of several other students also falling to the floor crying out in the agony of repentance needing prayer, and then one of them started writhing around on the floor as a demon manifested.

Those of us who knew what was going on joined with the visiting evangelist and the president of the Bible College to pray for the young man until the demon was cast out of him and then we prayed for the others as well. It was pretty chaotic for a while, but eventually things calmed down. The president of the College dismissed the class with the promise that the next day he would explain to everyone what had happened.

After the class, I was called aside to face the person most responsible for the quenching of the Holy Spirit in the school. He told me in front of the President of the Bible College that he did not even know if what happened was of God or not, but if I wanted to stay at the school, I would have to stand before the class the next day and apologize for not submitting to authority. If I prophesied again during the rest of the school year, I would be expelled.

I listened for God's guidance for the right response. I did not want to be expelled, but I was in too far to back out now if God wanted me out. "Submit to them" the Lord said, "but give them a message". I looked the man in the eyes and told him that I would submit to all that he asked and leave it up to God to judge between me and him. I told him that if what he is doing is right, God will bless it, but if not, it will all crumble to nothing. The man was seething, but did not say anything else and we all parted company on that note.

The next day I apologized to the class, not for the prophecy that God gave me, but for not submitting to those who were in authority over me. The rest of the semester went pretty well without incident. It was as spiritually dry as a graveyard, but I graduated along with the rest of the class, short of one student who ended up in a psych ward and another who later committed suicide.

The following year the College moved to a new location on the other side of town. Sometimes a few of us would audit a class when a guest speaker was there, but it was never the same again as it had been in the beginning. My heart sank a little when I heard that the school had moved to the a larger city for bigger and better opportunities.

I was further saddened but not surprised to hear that a short time later the school had closed. Now here we are many years later. The unfortunate state of affairs is that a large proportion of the people who attended the Bible College throughout the latter years are not even following the Lord any more. It should serve as a warning to others about how much we need the Holy Spirit to help and guide us if we want to keep serving God.

> How foolish can you be? After starting your new lives
> in the Spirit, why are you now trying to become perfect
> by your own human effort?
> Galatians 3:3 NLT

GOD CALLS ME TO GUATEMALA

Once Bible College was over, then came the dilemma of what to do next. I already told you the story of finding the missionary in Guatemala. Now let me tell you how I got there in the first place. Often missionary evangelists will have a chance to be the guest speakers at Bible Colleges as an opportunity to speak about their missions work in various countries. There was one visiting evangelist in particular who had inspired me to make a month long trip to Guatemala to see if I could help some of the Christian workers there in some small way.

Ironically, it was the same minister who had spoken on the day that I had gotten in so much trouble with the Bible school. Now I was certain that God wanted me to make the missions trip. Also, for some unknown reason I was convinced that I had to go right away after Bible College, as soon as possible without delaying.

I talked with my pastor and he put me in contact with a couple of groups in Guatemala City who offered me a place to stay while I was there and informed me that there was always need down there for children's clothing and medical supplies, mentioning that eye droppers, vitamins and aspirin in particular were in short supply. I told them that I would do my best to try to bring some of those things with me.

I called a travel agent to put a deposit down and book my flight, giving me about a month to raise funds and donated items for the trip. Fortunately, I already had two large steamer trunks that would be perfect for holding the children's clothing and medical supplies. All God had to do was help me fill them.

ASK AND YOU SHALL RECEIVE

One thing that I have learned over the years is that if we put our faith in God, He will give us favor with people to accomplish His work. As soon as I informed the pastor that the trip was arranged, the church took up an offering and over six hundred dollars was raised to be dispersed in Guatemala at my discretion. Then I went to a local thrift store and informed them of my mission. They gave me permission to take as much children's clothing as I wanted, so I was able to fill one entire steamer trunk with children's clothing for free.

Following that, I went to a medical supply place and they donated several boxes each containing twelve dozen eye droppers and many other valuable medical items such as thermometers, tongue depressors and some of their old stock of limb braces, all for free. Finally I went to a local pharmacy who provided me with a generous supply of aspirin and vitamins for a very nominal fee well below wholesale. I was ready to go, all except for one big problem. I needed $2500 to cover my plane ticket and my own living costs while I was down there. That would prove to be a real challenge.

GOD PROVIDES TO MEET OUR NEEDS

I had devised a plan that I had thought was more than sufficient to cover my own needs for the trip. I decided that I was willing to give up my camper van, my travel trailer and a near new air conditioner to cover my costs. As soon as I booked the flight I put ads in the newspapers offering all of these items at really low prices to make sure that they all sold. The van and trailer were worth $2500 each and I was only asking half of that so I did not think there would be a problem selling the items to raise the money. Three weeks later I had still been unable to sell a single item. With only a week to go, I had not even paid for my flight yet. I was getting desperate. Believe me when I say that my prayer time went into high gear.

Then one day I got a phone call. A man was offering me half of what I was asking for the air conditioner, which was about a quarter of what it was worth. I decided that selling it that cheaply would not get me much closer to my goal than not selling it at all. I assured the man of the quality of the unit and convinced him to come and have a look at it for the price that I was asking.

A short while later, the man arrived. He asked if I was a Christian because he had noticed the JESUS IS LORD bumper sticker on the back of the camper van. That started a conversation about why I was selling the air conditioner and the fact that I was also selling the camper van and travel trailer to pay for the costs of my trip. The man remarked that the Camper van was reasonably priced and asked to see it. Then he asked to see the trailer as well.

I had been trying unsuccessfully for weeks to sell these items on my own, and then God brought me one man in one day who listened to my testimony about what I believed God was calling me to do, and in the end he bought everything I had for the exact amount that I needed to raise to pay my expenses for the trip. God has His ways of working things out.

I showed up at the airport with a tiny carry on suitcase for my own belongings and two massive steamer trunks that were way over weight. I figured that I could buy whatever else I needed after I got there. I explained to the airline employees what I was doing. They passed me through with no extra charges for the grossly overweight luggage and I was on my way.

GOD CAN BLIND PEOPLE'S EYES
AND GIVE YOU FAVOR WITH MEN

When the plane set down in Guatemala City I headed for Customs and came face to face with the reality that I was not in Canada anymore. There were armed guards with shotguns and submachine guns everywhere and they all looked like they meant business. As I entered the long line up, I could see that absolutely every bag was being opened and checked. That made me real uneasy and put me into prayer mode with a furious intensity.

You have to realize how serious this situation was. Normally, it takes months to arrange this type of venture to a third world country. Permissions from government officials need to be granted and people need to be in the know about what is happening. I had none of that. All I had was a letter from one Christian organization verifying that I was coming to help them and would be staying with them.

I was entering a nation that was rampant with corruption on many different levels and I was bringing items into the country that were worth thousands of dollars on the black market. They could have demanded that I pay an exorbitant fee (bribe) before they would release anything. It was also possible that everything would be confiscated and I would be refused entry into the country and there would have been nothing that I could have done about it. Worse than that, they could have accused me of trying to smuggle contraband into the country and thrown me into jail. Again, there would have been nothing I could have done to stop it.

I began to pray with great intensity for God's protection and for God to give me favor with these people. When my turn came for my baggage to be examined I placed my small carry-on bag on the counter at the back, followed by the children's clothing. The most valuable and controversial trunk, the one with all of the medical supplies in it went on the counter at the front where it would likely be examined first.

For some reason the customs official started with the last item first. He dug thoroughly through my small bag, set it aside and then opened the steamer trunk full of children's clothes. As he rifled through all of the clothes I saw his face turn from normal to angry purple as he started rapidly shouting at me in Spanish, clearly thinking that I was trying to smuggle these items into the country and sell them.

This is not good, I thought. If they are this upset about children's clothing, what are they going to do when they get to the medical supplies valued at thousands of dollars? I prayed even harder as I attempted to explain things to him in my limited Spanish vocabulary. The armed guards were looking alert and way too interested in what was going on.

Then a more senior official was called over. I showed him the letter from the Christian organization indicating that I was coming to help them and explained to the official in what little Spanish I knew that the clothes were not going to be sold, but given to the orphans and poor children. The man looked me in the eyes for a moment, talked to his underlings and said one word to me "Passè", meaning go ahead, and he waved me toward the exit. Nobody seemed to notice that the third case had not been opened yet. It was like they didn't even see it, and I was certainly not going to point it out to them.

I quickly grabbed the unopened case containing the medical supplies and put it on the bottom of my luggage carrier. Nobody said anything. I closed up the trunk with the children's clothing and my carry-on bag and placed them on top. Then I headed for the door, still praying with all that was within me as I went. As I reached the door, someone coming through saw my white skin and asked "are you Michael Hunter from Canada?" It was my contact from the missionary organization. "Yes! Let's go, quickly", I said quietly.

After we got into the car, I filled him and his companions in on everything including the officials overlooking the trunk with the medical supplies and we all praised and thanked God that He had watched over me and the much needed items. It turned out that the fellow who picked me up did not even know for sure when I was going to be at the airport at that time. He had just showed up hoping that I would be there on that day.

GOD HAS GREAT TIMING, AGAIN

On the way back to the missionary base, I filled my hosts in on some of the items that I had brought with me and they were ecstatic about it. That very day, they were scheduled to go on a medical inoculation mission to the surrounding villages and many of the items that I had brought would prove to be useful.

When we arrived back at the compound we found that the bus was all loaded and ready to go but one of the tires that they had taken in to be fixed was unrepairable. It would have to be replaced but there was no money for the three hundred plus dollars that it would cost to replace the tire. Guess who had been given money for just such an emergency. In a short time they were on their way. Upon reporting back that evening they testified that many people had been helped medically and over sixty had given their heart to the Lord.

A lot of other wonderful things happened on that trip, but far too soon it was time to go home. A short time later I was back home in Kelowna again with a slide presentation and testimony of all the exciting things God had done on the trip to Guatemala. God did many wonderful things for me during the seven years between the day that I fully turned to Jesus and the time when I returned from my Missions trip. Most importantly, I knew that I was born again, a new creature in Christ Jesus and was now looking forward to whatever God had planned next for me as a Christian.

After arriving back in Kelowna I hosted numerous services in different places to tell of all the good things God had done and several people prophesied how God would continue to use me in mighty ways. Some of those prophecies have already come true, others may yet occur and some may never happen, but one in prophetic word particular rang true in my spirit, partly because it stood out from all the others.

The prophet said "I see you ministering the Word of the Lord to people in a small confined space." I was curious. I wondered what God meant by that one. It wasn't going to be very long before I found out what God was talking about.

CHAPTER 21

Don't Look at Circumstance

SATAN CAN USE OLD SINS
TO ATTACK AND TEST YOU

God had blessed me in many ways during the years between 1981 and 1988. I was saved and baptized in the Holy Spirit. I was delivered from financial debt. I had been physically healed from numerous ailments. I had witnessed God move supernaturally many times. I had seen my mother come to Jesus. I was a new person in Christ Jesus. I had even changed first name from Barry to Michael.

My legal name had always been Michael Barry, but for some reason, my parents had chosen to call me by my middle name, Barry. Then after I committed to the Lord in 1981 I discovered that the name Barry means "a spear". In a good connotation, one might think of a spear being a warrior's weapon. In my eyes, I saw my previous life to be like the guy who thrust a spear in the side of Jesus on the cross to make sure that He was dead. I chose that from that day forward, I would go by my real first name, Michael, which means "he who is like the Lord". Life was good. Things were going well.

Then it happened. Out of the blue, no later than a week after I returned from Guatemala I got a phone call from the police informing that I was going to be charged for an old crime that I had committed before I repented and came to the Lord in 1981.

This was something that I had done my best to reconcile and clear up back in 1981. I was told at the time that the victim was not pressing charges so I thought it was done with. Now seven years later the crown prosecutors had decided that they were going to proceed to prosecute me on their own accord. They said that due to the seriousness of the charges, they were going to make an example of me as a deterrent to others. God was about to allow my faith to be severely tested.

DON'T BLAME GOD FOR PROBLEMS
THAT WE CREATED.

Remember this. God will never do evil to you, neither will God ever tempt you to do evil. However, God will occasionally remove his protection from us and allow Satan to tempt us. Remember, it was Satan, not God, who tempted Adam and Eve in the Garden of Eden. It was Satan who afflicted Job, and it was Satan who tempted Christ in the wilderness after His baptism:

> And remember, when you are being tempted, do not say, "God is tempting me." God is never tempted to do wrong, and he never tempts anyone else. Temptation comes from our own desires, which entice us and drag us away. These desires give birth to sinful actions. And when sin is allowed to grow, it gives birth to death. James 1:13-15 NLT

When various trials and tribulations come our way in life Satan will often try to convince us that God is at fault and God is doing it to us. He'll try to convince us that God is punishing us for some reason. Remember, that's what he did to Job, and that's what he still does today.

Whenever trials come in life we must not undermine our own faith by falsely accusing God and asking God "why are you doing this to me?" There will also be times in our lives when we can't even fully blame Satan for our troubles because the things that we are suffering now are sometimes a product of our own past sins. In such cases, God expects us to suffer the consequences of our transgressions without complaining. Just keep serving the Lord, trusting that God will bring good out of the whole situation in the end.

> For what glory is it, if, when ye be buffeted for your faults, ye shall take it patiently? But if, when ye do well, and suffer for it, ye take it patiently, this is acceptable with God. 1 Peter 2:20 KJV

> And we know that all things work together for good to those who love God, to those who are the called according to His purpose. Romans 8:28 NKJV

> Do not fear any of those things which you are about to suffer. Indeed, the devil is about to throw some of you into prison, that you may be tested, and you will have tribulation ten days. Be faithful until death, and I will give you the crown of life. Revelation 2:10 NKJV

IT IS IMPORTANT TO KNOW
WHO YOUR ENEMY IS

When I was a young man I used to shake my fist at God and ask Him why He was doing this to me. Why was all this happening to me? Then Jesus and the Holy Spirit came into my life and I finally realized that I am my own worst enemy. I was the one responsible for many of the problems in my life. Furthermore, I now understand that any trials that I am not directly responsible for are caused by an even nastier enemy, Satan, and those he commands.

It was Satan who tried to take my life in the car crash in 1972. It was Satan who tried to take my life in the fire in 1984, and now after serving the Lord for seven years, there was no question in my mind that it was Satan who was manipulating circumstances to try to turn me against God in 1988, but I no longer believe the Devil. I believe God.

All of the thoughts and accusations were still showing up in my head, fighting for dominance. "You have served God for seven years and what good did it do?" "God doesn't care about you!" "Where is your God now?" "You're going to prison where you belong and God won't help you there!"

However, the one thing that Satan had not counted on in all of this was that I was no longer a slave to sin. I no longer believed His lies and I now trusted that God would be in control no matter what the outcome of this present trial was. Jesus Christ had truly set me free, and in prison or out of prison I was going to continue to serve the Lord.

The truth was that I was guilty and I knew that I deserved to go to prison for the things that I had done, but I also knew that God was now my Father, I was His Son and I would continue to be free even in prison if it came to that. I also knew that the only reason that God was allowing this to happen after seven years of serving Him was that He had a purpose in it all. If I was going to prison, God wanted me there. All I had to do was discover what it was that God wanted me to do while I was there. In prison or out of prison, I knew I would still continue to be a free man as long as I followed and served Jesus Christ.

> ...Jesus said, "If you hold to my teaching, you are really my disciples. Then you will know the truth, and the truth will set you free...Jesus replied, "Very truly I tell you, everyone who sins is a slave to sin. Now a slave has no permanent place in the family, but a son belongs to it forever. So if the Son sets you free, you will be free indeed. John 8:31-36 NIV

CHAPTER 22

From Pulpit to Prison

I FIND YOU GUILTY

The trial was the hardest thing. I never tried to deny anything or blame anybody and the requirement to stand publicly before people and state that I was guilty broke my heart all over again. When I uttered the plea of guilty, all of the pain and shame and regret and guilt and condemnation regarding the person I used to be came rushing back. I broke down on the stand for a few moments and the judge waited for me to regain my composure before continuing.

The prosecution was pushing for the maximum penalty without sending me to federal prison, a sentence of two years less a day. The only thing that I had in my favor was a huge stack of references from pastors, employers, landlords, friends, even a parole officer that I had been working with to help young offenders, all testifying that I was a different person now, not the same person who was once a criminal.

The judge told me that he believed that I was remorseful and unlikely to reoffend. He said he was moved to leniency by the letters that he had read about the change in my character. However, this did not alter the fact that I was guilty. As a deterrent to others he was sentencing me to eight months in maximum security at Prince George Regional Correctional Facility to begin immediately. I would go directly to prison from the courtroom.

Once the sentence was handed down, I was not really discouraged. I was actually relieved. The stress of not knowing what was going to happen was finally gone. It was like a huge burden had been lifted from my shoulders and I trusted that if I was going to prison, it was because God wanted me there for some reason. I was ready for whatever was coming.

I was taken directly from the courtroom to the Sherriff's van. There I had to face the added humiliation of being driven to prison by a female Sherriff who knew me. I even once had a crush on her in high school. I could have let it get me down. Instead, I turned the five hour van ride into an opportunity to admit my guilt to her and witness to my captive audience of all of the things that God had done since I gave my heart to Him. I have not seen her since, but I know that she was going through some trials of her own at the time. I believe that some of the things that I said to her touched her heart for Jesus.

SOME OF YOU WILL BE
CAST INTO PRISON

I am not sure what the new facility is like now, but the Provincial Correctional facility I was sent to was certainly no country club prison. It was a formidable place surrounded with high chain link fences topped with razor wire. When I arrived, all of my belongings except for my Bible were confiscated and stored and the Bible itself was carefully checked for any anomalies.

All of the new prisoners were given an orange shirt and pants, pair of underwear, pair of slippers and we were all ushered into a room where we had to strip and submit to a cavity search to ensure that no one was hiding anything in any opening on our bodies. Then we were taken toward our cells.

I was pulled aside by the warden and told that I was scheduled for the maximum security section, but due to overcrowding, he asked if I was willing to be put into the general population wing. This prison was a facility built for 150 prisoners and it was really overcrowded. At the time there were about 300 inmates who were incarcerated there and the maximum security wing was right full with double occupancy.

I didn't know why he chose me to do this, but I told the warden that

I would be willing to do whatever he wanted and was going to do my best to stay out of trouble. I only asked that I would have the option of moving to maximum security at a future date if it looked like there was going to be trouble that I could not avoid in the general population wing. He agreed and I got my first inside look at prison life.

The beds in general population were steel bunks with three inch mattresses that kept you away from the cold steel but offered little comfort. The biggest culture shock was that there was no privacy anywhere there, not even in the showers or toilets. The cell doors were left open unless there was a lockdown for some reason. It was certainly a place where you had to be aware of your surroundings and watch your back.

Was I afraid? No, not really. I wasn't careless, but I chose to believe that God had me there for a reason and I knew that God was well able to protect me even in there if He chose to do so. I will say, though, I was prayerful in everything I did and said and remained in constant prayer for the Holy Spirit to give me the wisdom and discernment of how to deal with any potential dangers that might arise. Prison is no joke.

Let me tell you this. If you want to learn how to pray with sincerity and intensity, prison is one place where you learn how to do it if you want to survive unscathed, although I hope no one reading this book ever has to go there. Hopefully most people reading this book will learn to pray and live for God without ever having to go to prison.

Even though I knew that my own past sins and Satan had put me in prison, I believed that God was going to use this for His good, so my main goal as soon as I got to the penitentiary was to try to discover what it was that God wanted me to do while I was in there. Then I would be able to make the most I could out of the situation that I was in. I was really at peace about the whole thing. God's Word reminded me that there was a peace of God that transcends all understanding for those who learn to trust God:

> Rejoice in the Lord always. I will say it again: Rejoice!
> Let your gentleness be evident to all. The Lord is near. Do
> not be anxious about anything, but in every situation,
> by prayer and petition, with thanksgiving, present your
> requests to God. And the peace of God, which transcends

all understanding, will guard your hearts and your minds in Christ Jesus. Finally, brothers and sisters, whatever is true, whatever is noble, whatever is right, whatever is pure, whatever is lovely, whatever is admirable—if anything is excellent or praiseworthy—think about such things. Whatever you have learned or received or heard from me, or seen in me—put it into practice. And the God of peace will be with you.

Philippians 4:4-9 NIV

DON'T BE ASHAMED OF ME

One thing that I understood was that if I was going to get out of prison in one piece, it was only going to be by the grace of God so I was not about to hide my faith from the other prisoners. Neither was I going to tarnish my Christianity to fit in with the crowd. The first thing that happened when I was shown to my bunk was that I opened my Bible, read a few verses, kneeled down and prayed quietly to the Lord.

I wanted to send a message to the other prisoners that this is who I was. Then I got up and walked through the place to check it over and look for a friendly face. A couple of guys invited me to join in on a cribbage game so I sat down and they filled me in on the routine.

Food was brought in three times a day and the tables we were using for entertainment were also our dining tables. There was one TV with a couple of channels and a few benches for common viewing. When the weather was good prisoners were allowed out in the exercise yard for a few hours each day. There was also the option twice a week to go to the gym for an hour or spend the same amount of time doing arts and crafts.

I was told that everyone eventually gets assigned to the laundry, the kitchen or the tailor shop for four hours a day. For their service in the work detail everyone got a few dollars a day to save or spend at the commissary for treats.

Once every two weeks the Catholic priest would hold services in the chapel and on the opposite Sunday the Protestants would hold their services. Lights out was at ten o'clock whether you liked it or not and if you wanted breakfast you had to be up early. The food wasn't actually that bad, not as bad as hospital food on the outside. Of course there were the ever present guards night and day to keep things under control.

It wasn't long before the conversation turned to why I was in there. Everybody wants to know why everyone else is in the prison, partly out of curiosity and partly to figure out where you fit in the prison hierarchy and class system. I told my story to my captive listeners whenever someone would ask.

One of the things that surprised me was the large number of inmates who were serving two years less a day just for alcohol related charges. It was a sobering thought when I contemplated that I had driven drunk many, many times during my early life. I was even caught a few times, but I had never been charged. I realized that for that crime alone I deserved to be there just as much as any of those men did, and I only had an eight month sentence for my crimes.

This only strengthened my resolve even more to find out why God wanted me there. Others were in there for theft or weapons offenses or violence or sexual misconduct and I had been guilty of all of those things at some time or other during my life. Rather than complain about the time I did get, I considered myself fortunate that I was only facing an eight month sentence. It could have been much longer, or it could have been federal prison.

Whenever someone tried to protest their innocence to me while I was there, I pointed out to them that all of our sentences would be a lot longer if we had been convicted of all of the things that we did do and got away with it. I explained to them that the important thing was to just do the time and not go back into that same old evil lifestyle again when we got out.

FISHING FOR WEEKS AND NO BITES

The Bible tells us that some of Christ's disciples were originally fishermen. Then Jesus told them to follow Him, saying He would make them fishers of men. Now there I was fishing for souls in prison and I hardly got a nibble for the first couple of weeks. Then one day, one of my cribbage partners confided that he would be getting out in a week. He had been in contact with professing Christians before, both in and out of the joint and he had never been impressed with them because they did not seem much different than he was.

He said he knew there was something different about me and he really wanted what I had. He wanted to change his life when he got out. So for the next week I took him through the basics of repentance and accepting Christ and did my best to answer all of his questions about God and God's Word. The day that he left, he thanked me and told me that he was going to find a good church and start attending it. Then the man was gone and the Devil started stirring up trouble in earnest.

SATAN DOES NOT LIKE
TO LOSE SOULS

I prayed and read my Bible every day in my cell when I was incarcerated and I know fully well that it was God's warriors (the Angels of God) who were my ultimate protection while I was in prison. Yet I was not about to give the impression to anyone that I was going to be an easy target either. I have had several years of martial arts training and practiced my martial arts katas in my cell as a good way to keep in shape as well as an advertisement to the other inmates.

I was also quite strong for my size. In the weight room, I made sure that others were watching as I did leg presses with over four hundred pounds of weight on the other end. It was partly for exercise, but partly to suggest to other individuals that maybe you should not try to cause trouble with this guy. However, there are lots of big strong men in prison, so you still need to be alert and careful every day. I knew that ultimately only God could guarantee my safety.

In addition, if you want to stir up a hornet's nest in your life, just start reaching out to people for Jesus. The Devil hates to lose souls and he will soon go to work to try to shut you up for good. There was one prisoner in particular who did not like me or the fact that I was a Christian. I was not concerned about him by himself because he had the demeanor of a coward, but once the fellow that I had been witnessing to left, this other guy started stirring up some of the other prisoners and making threats against my life, saying that that him and his friends were all going to get me one day.

In case you think that I am exaggerating the risk, BC Corrections Services data recorded over 800 inmate on inmate assaults at that particular prison during the six year period between 2004 and 2010 and seventy assaults against staff during the same period.

I prayed to the Lord about what to do regarding these threats. I felt assured that I had been faithful to God and that the man that I was supposed to talk to was now gone, so I went to the warden and let him know what was going on. Thankfully, the warden agreed to transfer me into the maximum security wing of the prison within the next couple of days and the transfer happened before anything came to a violent head.

MAXIMUM SECURITY, PRISON IS NO PICNIC

In the maximum security wing that I was now headed for, one of the inmates had just been re-integrated back into the wing after a week in isolation for seriously assaulting another inmate and all privileges had been temporarily revoked until things settled down again. I repeat, prison is no joke, my friends. It's a dangerous place. Be wiser than I was. If you have not been living for God, start now. If you don't believe anything else I tell you, trust me. You will not enjoy prison.

When you look at things from a natural perspective, it might seem like I was going from the frying pan into the fire. This was where all the high risk offenders were. There were murderers, violent offenders and sexual offenders waiting to be remanded to Federal prison for long-term sentences, and this is where the judge had determined I must be.

I now believe that it was the Lord who had influenced the warden to put me in the general population for a couple of weeks, just so God could use me to talk to that one man. There were also firebugs in maximum security and mentally unstable people with psychosis problems who wandered around muttering to themselves for a good part of the day. Often, violence could erupt at the slightest real or imagined provocation.

There was one fellow in particular who would often pace back and forth in the common area jabbering to himself or some unseen spiritual tormentor. Suddenly, he would just stop, stare someone in the eye and declare "I would rather burn than fade away!" Then he would resume his pacing and babbling. There were other people who were there for their own protection because, for whatever reasons they were not safe in the general population.

In spite of the seriousness of the crimes of some of the inmates in Maximum, prisoners were generally somewhat safer in the Maximum wing than they were in general population because security was a lot tighter in there. There were more guard checks and one was always stationed just outside the locked door of the common area to keep an eye on things. There were less privileges though. You only got one hour of exercise time a day. There were also two prisoners per eight by ten cell and every cell was locked from ten at night till six in the morning.

That means that you had better hope that you get along with your cellmate in Maximum Security because you are locked in there with them for eight hours every night. If you had a good cellmate, you were actually safer at night than in general population. If not, things could go badly for you before the guard ever got to you.

I am certain they have toilets in the cells now, but not when I was there. If you had to use the washroom during the night, too bad for you. If you were desperate enough, there was a steel bucket under your bed that you could use. Then you would get the dubious privilege of washing it out yourself the next morning if you had to use it during the night.

To give you an idea how small these cells were, the beds took up half the space. That leaves about four feet by ten feet for two people. That's only four steps from one end of the cell to the other and there is hardly enough room to walk past each other if you are both standing in the cell at the same time. There is nothing to do in your cell but sit or lay on your bed day or night. You can't even read at night because there are no lights after ten. I heard more than one man who thought he was a tough guy cry himself to sleep at night while I was in there.

FRIENDLY FACES IN HARD PLACES

The moment I entered the cell block in Maximum, I was surprised to see a familiar friendly face from my home church. He was a genuinely nice guy who professed to be a Christian but he was a person of diminished mental capacity. I found out later that he had gotten himself in trouble due to the dangerous combination of adult sexual urges combined with the mind and lack of moral compass of a preschooler.

I had always treated him kindly on the outside so he was really glad to see me and immediately offered to let me have the empty bunk in his cell. There wasn't any other choice anyway. It was the only empty bunk in the whole wing.

The guy was eager to have some friendly company so I was happy to bunk with him, although I wondered why the only spare bed was in the cell of this really nice fellow when all the other cells were full. Overcrowding was obviously a problem in Maximum Security as well as in the general population so I was fortunate to get a bed there at all, but I wondered why such a friendly guy didn't have a cell mate.

We talked for hours about why I was there and why he was there and I strongly encouraged him in simple terms that we both had to repent and live our lives completely for Jesus so that we would never have to come back to a place like this. We read my Bible and prayed together until lights out. About ten minutes later I found out why this guy had no cellmate. He snored like somebody revving a motorcycle with no baffles in the muffler and he did it all night long.

When this fellow was sleeping you could clearly hear him all the way at the other end of the cell block and now I was stuck with him in an eight by ten steel speaker box every night for eight hours. I hardly slept at all for the first two days until someone else was released and I was able to move into a cell with another professing Christian about half way down the cell block. Then the next newbie would have to go through the initiation of trying to sleep in that other cell. Fortunately, my former cell mate was understanding about why I had to move and we both remained good friends during my stay there.

ARE THERE PROFESSING CHRISTIANS IN PRISON?

It might surprise you to know that there are actually quite a few. Some become Christians while they are in prison, but the majority are there because they were never taught repentance as an essential component of salvation. They thought that they would be able to claim that Jesus is Lord with their lips and still live for the Devil in their daily behavior, and now here they were in prison paying for their foolishness.

I was determined that before I left the prison I would do whatever I could to change that mindset among the professing Christians and change things for the better for those who were in there. I was also committed to the goal that by the time I left there would not be any professing Christian in that prison who was under the false impression that you could keep on sinning and still go to be with Jesus.

On several occasions I had to reprove some professing Christian for participation in unquestionably evil conduct. As with the general population wing, I never tried to push Christianity on anybody who did not want to listen, but anyone interested was able to hear the unfiltered story of how I ended up in prison and how God had changed my life.

Word gets around quickly in prison. Before long I found out that the Maximum Security population of 50 inmates contained about a half dozen professing Christians and a few more who were open to hearing about Christianity. They were all like sheep without a shepherd and they looked to me to help them. The Christian prisoners asked if I would be willing to set up a half hour daily bible study and teaching time for anyone who wanted to attend. I was happy to do so, concentrating mainly on repentance, faith in Jesus Christ and the other fundamentals of salvation and Christian discipleship.

By focusing on the basic principles of Salvation, I labored to ensure that all those who listened and believed God would have the best opportunity of success when they left prison. They would have a solid foundation of repentance and faith in the Rock of Jesus Christ upon which they could build the rest of their life. Thanks to these Bible studies and my witnessing during my time in prison I was able to lead two more people to accept Jesus Christ as their Savior. In addition, I believe that many more were influenced toward thinking about God and Salvation and I am sure that I will see at least some of them again when Jesus comes.

PHYSICAL HARDSHIPS AND
SOCIAL SECURITY

I found the steel prison bunks with almost no padding really hard on my back which made it difficult to sleep sometimes. This problem was further complicated by the fact that a couple of months into my sentence I injured my ribs playing volleyball during exercise time. Injured ribs are something that take three or four weeks to heal and the doctors can't really do much to help anything.

For a while, I was so sore that I could not even sit up to get out of bed. I had to roll over, drop my feet off the edge and sort of push myself to a standing position using my leg muscles and my arms. All I could do was wait for them to heal on their own. For the first while, even coughing or sneezing was agony for me and that steel bunk did not help matters at all.

On the other hand, I found that in the Maximum wing even the non-Christian inmates were often easier to get along with than those in general population. It turned out that the inmates had a lot of respect for me because I was honest and transparent with everybody, not like the phony Christians that they were used to encountering. Over time, opportunities arose to talk with many of these troubled men about God.

There was one big First Nations fellow in particular who stood head and shoulders above the others, and I mean literally. He was about six foot four, three hundred pounds and was in the Maximum Security wing on remand awaiting transfer to federal prison for an alcohol related triple murder.

This was the guy who had just returned from solitary confinement after putting the hurt on a fellow prisoner a couple of days before I arrived. As far as I know, this was the biggest guy in the whole place and for some reason he took a liking to me. I believe that God gave me favor with the man.

There is a lot of spare time in prison so we'd often play a variety of board games as we talked. He'd complain and throw a tantrum sometimes when he lost, but I think that he respected that I wasn't really afraid of him and consequently would not let him win all the time when we were playing. I'm pretty sure that he would have had my back if anyone had tried anything against me, particularly while I was nursing the injured ribs.

I socialized with this man a lot, talking about life and God while I was there. He never accepted Christ while I was there but we spent a lot of free time together and I was pretty grateful that God had given me a wingman who was built like the famous wrestler Andre the Giant. Besides, who knows what may come of it all in the end? He was facing a possibility of life in prison for his sins, but maybe in the end, like the thief on the cross, I'll see him in heaven. I truly hope so.

WORKING FOR CHRIST IN
THE PRISON SYSTEM

I was determined to do more than just serve my time while I was in prison. I firmly believed that the Lord had me there for a reason, so I looked for opportunities to make positive changes wherever that was possible. I had noticed that the Catholic priest appeared to be a very devout man genuinely concerned about the spiritual welfare of the inmates. In addition to his services every second Sunday, he also spent a lot of quality time visiting the men and encouraging them during the week.

I was not very happy about the idea of only having church every second Sunday, so I asked the priest if he would mind if the Protestant inmates attended his Sunday services. He was a pretty open-minded guy. He was so thrilled with the idea that when we all showed up, he loaned me his guitar and allowed me to lead the praise and worship services.

I don't know if the practice of attending services every week continued after I left, but I hope that it did. I am far less concerned about a little Catholic tradition rubbing off on an inmate than I am about one going to hell because no one ever warned them that they have to repent and accept Jesus as their Savior if they want to go to heaven.

The other thing that concerned me about the prison system was that there was a library which contained plenty of magazines and novels containing violence and questionable sexual morality. There were even more than a few horror novels, but there were only a few Bibles and there was virtually no solid Christian reading material. After talking with the warden, I obtained permission to phone back to some friends in Kelowna and have them bring up a big stack of uplifting Christian books for the library to help the inmates learn more about Christianity and about growing in faith and obedience to God. One more opportunity to reach out for Jesus.

THREE MONTHS IN THE JOINT
AND UP FOR PAROLE

In the Canadian correctional system, unless there are extenuating circumstances, once an inmate has served a third of their sentence, you become eligible for parole but it is certainly no guarantee that you will be let out. When I was brought before the Parole Board, I did not expect to make parole. Some serious crimes had recently been committed by parolees in the area. There was political pressure being applied to try to tighten up the parole system. Considering the seriousness of the charges and the fact that almost no paroles were going through at the time, things did not look very optimistic for any kind of early release for me, so I was expecting the worst.

After the meeting with the parole officers was over they asked me to wait outside while they held a private discussion. When I was called back in I was a little shocked to hear their decision. After serving only three months of my sentence, I was going to be released on probation for two years. During that period I would have to report regularly to a probation officer, attend psychological counselling and stay out of trouble. After that, I would be a free man, although I would be a man with a prison record.

The parole officers wished me luck and expressed that they hoped that they would never see me again. It took another few days to take care of the paperwork and at last my time in prison was over. I said my goodbyes to everyone inside and was escorted out of the facility. My body was once again as free as my spirit.

When they booked me out, I was grateful to see that some Christian friends showed up on my release date to give me a ride back home to Kelowna. Looking back on it now, I think that one of the reasons that I got the early parole was that the Devil just wanted me out of there before I did any more damage to his kingdom.

CHAPTER 23

Return to Ministry

GOD RESTORES MY LIFE

I have never regretted or resented God for requiring me to go to prison for a time. To begin with, I know it was a test and the truth is that I deserved to be there as much as anyone else who was in there. Being required to pay my debt to society for at least some of my sins has also helped me to achieve closure on that part of my life. Plus, it was in prison that I first had the honor of personally leading other people to accept Jesus Christ as their Savior.

Before that time I had witnessed to many people about accepting Christ over the years. I had directed seekers to churches and other church leaders who then led them to accept Jesus. However, it was not until I went to prison that I personally led anyone to accept Jesus Christ as their Savior. To this very day this has become a precious memory to me. Upon returning to the outside, it was then a bit of a shock to discover that a few supposedly mature professing Christians distanced themselves from me and treated me coldly and unkindly after I got out of prison.

There were also false rumors circulated by some who did not know the whole story. It hurt that these false rumors were instrumental in generating an atmosphere of fear and mistrust amongst those who chose to believe them, but the Lord assured me that these would be healed in time as long as I remained faithful to Him. There were far more Christians who were kind and helpful to me as I set out on my new life for God, now unhindered by the chains of my past.

One of the stipulations of parole was that I was required to have a supervised place to stay until my parole was up. A faithful and kind retired Christian couple rented me their basement suite until the requirements of my parole were complete and I was finally free to live on my own.

Being required to visit the secular psychologist and report to the parole officer was inconvenient and a little frustrating because of their secular philosophies and perspectives on life, but I chose to look at it as an opportunity to witness to two more people about how Jesus Christ has changed my life and I am not the same person that I used to be.

I actually stayed in contact with the parole officer for several years afterward regarding ongoing rehabilitation and Christian counselling that I was doing to help young offenders and adults who were going through some of the same things that I had gone through.

My former pastor in Kelowna warmly welcomed me back into his fellowship where I gladly sat and ministered under His headship for many years. There was also a Christian organization that (in spite of my past) sponsored me for my ministry license and ordination. Then there was the Christian Minister's Association who accepted me as a pastoral member, and I have remained with this Association now for over 30 years.

Since then I have ministered in several different ways in numerous different locations, sometimes as a senior pastor and sometimes as an associate pastor. Not once have I ever wanted to go back to my former life. Yet there were certainly times during my first thirteen years serving God that I wished that the Lord would help me with my loneliness. I still longed to love and be loved.

I LEARNED THAT GOD IS ALL I NEED

One of the greatest challenges that I have ever had to face in life is loneliness. From my early youth I had always wanted to love and be loved and share my life with someone but Satan had used pornography and my own lusts to steal that from me. As a young man I thought that the solution to my loneliness was to find a wife and raise a family, but that did not solve my problem because my real problem was more complicated than that. It was a sin problem.

I have since learned that without God there is a hole in our lives that cannot be filled with anything else that exists on Earth. Wealth and fame cannot fill it. Marriage and children cannot fill it. However, evil will find a way into that hole in our lives if we allow it to, and then evil will steadily work toward destroying us.

Once I truly understood that I was created by God to love and be loved by God first, the Holy Spirit started pushing the evil and the loneliness out of that hole in my life. I realized that God was all I really needed to experience a joyous and fulfilling life on Earth until Jesus returns to take me away or I die and pass on to Heaven before that day comes.

I finally reached a place of contentment in my life that if it was God's will for me to remain single for the rest of my life, I was happy with that. No matter what, for the rest of my life I wanted to continue to serve the Lord, alone if necessary. Whatever He had for me, I reached a point where I was content to follow after Jesus as my Savior.

> My son, do not forget my teaching, but keep my commands in your heart, for they will prolong your life many years and bring you peace and prosperity. Let love and faithfulness never leave you; bind them around your neck, write them on the tablet of your heart. Then you will win favor and a good name in the sight of God and man. Trust in the LORD with all your heart and lean not on your own understanding; in all your ways submit to him, and he will make your paths straight. Do not be wise in your own eyes; fear the LORD and shun evil. This will bring health to your body and nourishment to your bones.
> Proverbs 3:1-8 NIV

Ever since my conversion in 1981, the main focus of my life has now been to take what God has given to me and pass it on to others. I work at a secular job to put food on the table and a roof over our heads, but I live to tell other people about Jesus Christ in the hope that through my testimony and my teaching God will be gracious and save others as well. It has been prophesied that I will touch people around the world and I believe that this is a true word from God. Maybe this book is a step in that direction.

GOD RESTORED WHAT
SATAN HAD STOLEN

I had reached the state of spiritual maturity where I was content to serve God as I was. Then one day God also gave me an added blessing. Her name is Leigh Ann. Nine years after I met her, God opened my eyes to view this precious and beautiful young woman that I had seen in Kelowna on the first day of Bible College in a new and different way. From the very beginning I had noticed that she embodied the wonderful gentle spirit of a godly woman and we had become close friends over the years. Leigh Ann wrote to me when I was in prison. She had encouraged me to continue to have faith in God and her letters had been a great blessing to me, but we had always been just good friends.

Then came the day when Leigh Ann was at my mother's side holding her hand when Mom passed on to be with Jesus. As I watched my Mom's spirit fade away and head for the glories of Heaven in 1994, the Lord said "this is the wife whom I have chosen for you." We were married that same year and Leigh Ann has been my constant companion now for over twenty-five years. We both know that God is our Father and we are His children and soon our journey back to Father God will be complete.

God, my shepherd! I don't need a thing. You have bedded me down in lush meadows, you find me quiet pools to drink from. True to your word, you let me catch my breath and send me in the right direction. Even when the way goes through the Valley of Death, I'm not afraid when you walk at my side. Your trusty shepherd's crook makes me feel secure. You serve me a six-course dinner right in front of my enemies. You revive my drooping head; my cup brims with blessing. Your beauty and love chase after me every day of my life. I'm back home in the house of God for the rest of my life. Psalm 23 MSG (paraphrased).

In 2004 I applied for and received a pardon from the Canadian government for my past crimes, putting the final nail in the coffin of my past life. However, I still have to pay a three hundred dollar waiver application every two years if I want to the U.S. because their laws are different. Other than that God has closed the door on my criminal record and I am grateful for that. All throughout my former life I never was free. I never was independent. I thought that I was, but I started out as a prisoner of Satan which resulted in me becoming a prisoner of the Law. I never really was free. Now I am a servant of Jesus Christ. The apostle Paul referred to it as being a prisoner for Christ, and I have never felt freer in my life.

CHAPTER 24

The Way Of Salvation

WOULD YOU LIKE TO RECEIVE JESUS CHRIST AS YOUR SAVIOR?

This is my first book. I believe that there will be others, but this book will not be complete if I do not pass on the opportunity for every reader to receive the wonderful gift of eternal life that God has given to me through repentance and faith in Jesus Christ as my Savior.

I love God. He is my true Father in heaven and my spirit soars whenever I spend time with Him. I would not trade my relationship with Jesus Christ for anything this world has to offer. I am looking forward to His coming and I want to go with Him when He comes. If I have one desire above all other things in this world dear reader, it is my hope that when I get to heaven, you too will be there.

God's Word tells us that Father God is a loving, forgiving and merciful Lord who does not condemn us. The whole world is condemned already due to the evil that is inherent in humanity as a result of Adam's choice to welcome it into human nature. God does not want that for us. God's desire is to save us from this state of eternal servitude to Satan that mankind is presently in bondage to.

For this purpose Father God sent His Word to Earth to become the only begotten sinless Son Jesus Christ, taking the penalty for our sin upon

Himself. Jesus Christ willingly submitted to death to pay the penalty for Adam's rebellion, to pay the penalty for all of mankind's sins.

For that selfless act of love, Father God raised Jesus Christ from the grave and has declared Him to be the only Savior of the entire world. Jesus Christ is the fulfilment of God's promise to the first two human beings (Adam and Eve) that one of Eve's descendants would become the Redeemer of the human race, offering Salvation to all who choose to turn away from evil and accept God's Redeemer as their Savior.

DO YOU WANT ASSURANCE
THAT YOU ARE SAVED?

Many people in the world today live in fear of God and fear of coming judgement because of ongoing sin in their lives, but it does not have to be that way. God has shown us the path of Salvation and all we have to do is take it. Just repent. Stop doing evil. Depart from iniquity and accept Jesus Christ as our Savior instead of choosing to continue to walk in disobedience to Jesus Christ.

> Enter through the narrow gate. For wide is the gate and broad is the road that leads to destruction, and many enter through it. But small is the gate and narrow the road that leads to life, and only a few find it... "Not everyone who says to me, 'Lord, Lord,' will enter the kingdom of heaven, but only the one who does the will of my Father who is in heaven. Many will say to me on that day, 'Lord, Lord, did we not prophesy in your name and in your name drive out demons and in your name perform many miracles?' Then I will tell them plainly, 'I never knew you. Away from me, you evildoers!' "Therefore everyone who hears these words of mine and puts them into practice is like a wise man who built his house on the rock. The rain came down, the streams rose, and the winds blew and beat against that house; yet it did not fall, because it had its foundation on the rock. But everyone who hears

these words of mine and does not put them into practice is like a foolish man who built his house on sand. The rain came down, the streams rose, and the winds blew and beat against that house, and it fell with a great crash." Matthew 7:13-27 NIV

I strongly urge you with tears. Don't let your house collapse as I once did. God promises us that the way to Salvation is not complicated. It is so simple that even a small child can understand it. All God asks of us is that we reject (repent from) evil thoughts speech and behavior in our lives.

We are all prodigal sons and daughters. All God wants us to do is turn away from darkness and come back to His light so that we can be part of His family again. God promises that if we repent and accept Jesus Christ as our Savior, Father God will adopt us back into His family again as His own sons and daughters.

DON'T BE PROUD.
ACCEPT GOD'S HELP

God has also given us the opportunity to receive His Holy Spirit to empower and help us to live our lives in a way that is pleasing to Our Father who is in Heaven. That's all there is to it. That's what it means to be "born again" by the Spirit of God. 1. Repent. 2. Believe. 3. Receive.

The reason that I stress the importance of being willing to receive the Holy Spirit is that God does not want you to go through the trials of life and the struggles against sin on your own. Some of you have probably tried to do that many times by yourself and failed over and over again, just like I once did. That's not the way God wants it to be. There is victory for you. God wants to help us overcome sin and be victorious over Satan. Receive the Holy Spirit and let Him help you.

God's Word tells us that if we have repented of our sins, accepted Jesus Christ as our Savior and are allowing the Holy Spirit to lead us toward God, we are spiritually born again. We are indeed saved. Yet, God's Word tells us that there is more to Christianity than just getting saved. Just as natural children need adults to love, care, protect, guide and help them grow to maturity, so do those who are newly born again in the spirit.

We need the help, protection, loving nurture and oversight of good Christian leadership if we are to grow into strong healthy mature Christians ourselves. Don't avoid or forsake going to a good Bible-believing church. True Christians know that going to church doesn't save us. We participate in Christian services because we believe God when He says that it will be beneficial for us.

We acknowledge that God has appointed leaders in the church to help us learn the meaning and value of water baptism and Communion. We know that God has put leaders in place to teach us about and the Holy Spirit and His gifts. We know they are there to help us grow and mature and bring us back to God's paths of righteousness whenever we stray from it.

Don't try to be a Christian all on your own. That's as abnormal as the thought of a newborn infant rejecting all contact from parents who want to feed, help, love and protect them from harm. Learn to trust the Word of God when it says that it is good for us to meet together regularly for corporate teaching and worship and prayer and fellowship. Find a Bible-believing church and go to it regularly.

God is our Father in Heaven. He has provided loving surrogate parents for us in the form of Bible-believing pastors and mature Christians. The Bible tells us that they are like shepherds of God's flocks and God has called them to take care of us and help us grow until we are mature enough to also bring others to the Lord and help them grow via a solid foundation of the Gospel of Jesus Christ.

Let's all work together for the common goal that when Jesus comes for His Bride, we will all clearly see the open door to heaven and enter in. Who in their right mind would want to find out the truth later by trying to get Jesus to re-open the door only to have Jesus Christ say "I do not know you. Depart from me evildoers and all who work iniquity."

My dear readers. We are at the midnight hour in the clock of human history. God is once again raising up prophets to warn the spiritual nation of Christianity to repent and come back to God. It is the end-times. There are many today who are blind and unconcerned about sin in the church, thinking that Jesus will overlook it all as long as we profess that "Jesus is

Lord". If that is what you have believed, you have believed a lie. It's a false gospel.

This book is only a small part of a cry that is beginning to go out worldwide to all who profess to know Jesus Christ as man's Savior. The parable of the ten virgins is not about Christians and non-Christians. Non-Christians are not looking for the coming of the Bridegroom. They think He's dead. In the parable of the ten virgins, they are **all** looking for the coming of the Bridegroom. They are all professing Christians, but Jesus said that five are wise and five are foolish. The wise will go with Jesus when He comes for His Bride. The foolish will be left behind to share the fate of the rest of those who have lived wickedly and refused to depart from their iniquities.

God wants us all to be wise and walking in the light when Jesus returns. I pray the love of God, the obedient example of Jesus Christ and the peace and joy of the Holy Spirit will guide you into all truth. Then if we are all still alive when the time comes, this Scripture will become a reality:

> But let me tell you something wonderful, a mystery I'll probably never fully understand. We're not all going to die—but we are all going to be changed. You hear a blast to end all blasts from a trumpet, and in the time that you look up and blink your eyes—it's over. On signal from that trumpet from heaven, the dead will be up and out of their graves, beyond the reach of death, never to die again. At the same moment and in the same way, we'll all be changed. In the resurrection scheme of things, this has to happen: everything perishable taken off the shelves and replaced by the imperishable, this mortal replaced by the immortal. Then the saying will come true:
> Death swallowed by triumphant Life!
> Who got the last word, oh, Death?
> Oh, Death, who's afraid of you now?
>
> It was sin that made death so frightening and law-code guilt that gave sin its leverage, its destructive power. But now in a single victorious stroke of Life, all three—sin,

guilt, death—are gone, the gift of our Master, Jesus Christ. Thank God! With all this going for us, my dear, dear friends, stand your ground. And don't hold back. Throw yourselves into the work of the Master, confident that nothing you do for him is a waste of time or effort.

1 Corinthians 15:51-58 MSG

Listen to me dear readers. We are not evolved from pond slime. We are not the next evolutionary step up the ladder from sub-apes. God created the human race as eternal beings who will only live out the first miniscule portion of our existence in these mortal bodies. Jesus said that these biological bodies which we all wear are only vessels, temples containing the spiritual offspring of God who we really are. Jesus told his enemies (speaking of His body) "You can destroy this temple, but I will raise it up again, and one day soon, Jesus is going to do that for us too.

The natural will become supernatural, mortality will become immortality and death will be no more. I am encouraged by God's promise that even if my body dies before that day, **I will never die**. Jesus Christ is coming back again, just as He said He would. Let's be ready when that day comes.

Your true friend and servant of Jesus Christ,
Michael Hunter

Printed in the United States
By Bookmasters